Surfing Your Career

Send for a free copy of the latest catalogue to:

How To Books
3 Newtec Place, Magdalen Road,
Oxford OX4 1RE
United Kingdom
info@howtobooks.co.uk
http://www.howtobooks.co.uk

Surfing Your Career

SECOND EDITION

HILARY NICKELL

howtobooks

Published by How To Books Ltd,
3 Newtec Place,
Magdalen Road,
Oxford OX4 1RE, United Kingdom
Tel: 01865 793806 Fax: 01865 248780
E-mail: info@howtobooks.co.uk
www.howtobooks.co.uk

All rights reserved. No part of this work may be reproduced
or stored in an information retrieval system (other than for
purposes of review), without the express permission of the
publisher in writing.

© Copyright 2002 Careers Management Ltd

1st edition 2000
2nd edition 2002

British Library Cataloguing in Publication Data.
A catalogue record for this book is available from
the British Library.

Cover design by Baseline Arts Ltd, Oxford

Produced for How To Books by Deer Park Productions
Typeset by PDQ Typesetting, Newcastle-under-Lyme, Staffs.
Printed and bound in Great Britain by Cromwell Press, Trowbridge, Wiltshire

Note: The material contained in this book is set out in good
faith for general guidance and no liability can be accepted for
loss or expense incurred as a result of relying in particular
circumstances on statements made in the book. Laws and
regulations are complex and liable to change, and readers
should check the current position with the relevant
authorities before making personal arrangements.

Contents

Preface

There is little doubt that the Internet offers exciting as well as limitless sources of information. Connect to any number of search engines with specific or general topics of interest and a feast of enticing delights await your surfing pleasure. The world of careers information and lifelong learning opportunities is also there to be explored. However, without help and in some instances professional guidance the process of tracking down the detail you need can be immensely frustrating, time consuming and costly.

This book is designed to help and encourage you, whether pursuing that first career goal, actively job seeking, or considering a change of profession. Alternatively you might be looking to broaden your educational experience or inspire that latent talent or interest. The Introduction explains the methods used to select and evaluate the quality of career information on the Internet, recognising that details constantly change and that the content can vary from being fully comprehensive to of little real value. A number of suggestions are listed to support your research and help you get all the information you need to make those important, but crucially informed decisions.

The ensuing occupational chapters provide a brief introduction to a broad range of related careers, describing the interests and skills that are often common to such professions, as well as details of the types of work they can include. Anyone who does not yet have a clear idea about which career path to follow, should find these sections helpful, if only at this stage, to eliminate certain careers and short list others for further enquiry. Each site is then listed according to whether it has particular points of specific interest or warrants star rated status on the basis of the quality and breadth of information included. (See the Introduction for more details of the selection criteria used.)

Few would argue that most successful career decisions are based upon having all the appropriate facts, and to this end well over 200 education and training web sites have been included to support your research (see Chapter 7). This is complemented by comprehensive job-hunting (Chapter 8), which includes guidance on CV and interview skills, as well as important additional information to help those with health problems or learning difficulties, or who are minority groups in society.

My hope is that this book will provide every reader with a massive dose of encouragement – that wherever you are on life's journey, there will be something to inspire those aspirations, hopes and dreams.

In loving memory of my mother Daphne, truly one of life's great encouragers!

Happy surfing!

Your comments on sites as well as suggestions for improvements in future editions will be warmly welcome. Please e-mail me at **hilary@surfin2careers.com**

Hilary Nickell

Introduction

SELECTION CRITERIA

Access to high-quality, up-to-date careers information has always been an important feature in professional guidance as well as essential support if individuals are to make realistic and informed decisions about their future. In one sense, the Internet is to be welcomed as it offers a treasure chest of almost limitless resources. However, there is also a potential problem: just because something is on the Internet does not mean it is of good quality or even accurate. In addition, outdated or incorrect information will at best waste valuable time, and at worst start off your new career or course of study on completely the wrong track. In order to help you avoid such difficulties, a star-rating system has been used for the main sites within all the major job categories. While some sites may not be comprehensive, they can still provide very useful, even essential information, and are therefore mentioned in the introductory comments or listed under 'other sites of interest'.

Star-Rating Evaluation
★★★ **Excellent**
A three-star rating is only awarded to high-quality sites offering comprehensive careers information and advice. It is likely that such sites will include **most** of the following:

- Equal opportunity statements and clear evidence of minority and disabled people being employed within the organisation.
- Up-to-date careers information, ideally with personal profiles and case studies of staff who are progressing through their chosen career, plus details of the different types of job roles within an organisation you may work for and the environment and skills required.
- Full explanation and advice on all appropriate education and training routes to the profession, as well as a commitment to continuing professional development (CPD).
- Information about the opportunities and prospects, late entry, as well as pay and conditions.
- Access to job-hunting information and, ideally, live vacancies.

- Occasionally sites will include helpful tips on interviews and CV preparation.

★★ Very good

Two-star sites will include **some** of the above comments and can satisfy **most** information needs.

★ Good

One-star sites can provide **essential help and advice**, but you may need to do additional research to get all the information you require.

You may occasionally come across duplicate site titles which have different star ratings. Which quality mark they warrant will largely depend on the specific nature of the careers information being assessed.

The reviews of, and comments about sites are, by necessity, 'snapshots' at the time of review. It would be unfair both to you, the readers, and to the publishers of sites not to point this out. Because the Internet has made publishing information so much easier and more dynamic, many sites will undergo minor, and sometimes major, changes between them being reviewed by me and you seeing them. So if you see a review that does not do a site justice, please accept my apologies or, better still, e-mail me and tell me what you think.

SELF-HELP GUIDE

While every effort has been made to evaluate and record the latest careers information on the Internet, you may still have interests or educational needs that have not yet made it to the pages of this book. Alternatively, you may have come across some great sites with masses of information but are looking for help to track down specific detail and also want to be sure of not missing anything that is particularly important.

This section is therefore designed to encourage you, whether you are a complete novice or an experienced user of the world wide web (www). We will look briefly at a number of search methods, explore some exciting short cuts to potential information gems and also check out some alternative sources of help.

Searching the Internet

If we can assume you have already checked the Contents page and more detailed Job Index at the back of this book, we can now try to track down potential information sources by using specific keywords. The next step is to place your keyword into the search facility on your computer, e.g. Freeserve, MSN or Yahoo to name but a few Internet Service Providers (ISPs). Your computer will now trawl cyberspace in a few seconds. You may be fortunate and find just what you are looking for quite quickly, but such a random form of searching is not always reliable. You can find yourself going up blind web alleys, not locating any sites, or discovering hundreds, or even thousands of Internet links, potentially wasting valuable time and money. A more successful method is to 'click' into the larger address box at the top of your Internet page (it turns blue), type www.name/subject or initial and close with one of the following more common endings:

.co.uk   **.org.uk**   **.com**
.gov.uk   **.ac.uk** (normally further and higher education sites)

This method can also be quite good fun, as it puts you in control and, providing your entries are not too obscure, should yield results. Be aware that **.org** and **.com** are commonly used by different countries.

The following examples show how this method works:

1. **Career example**
   http://www.plumbers.org.uk   The Institute of Plumbing

2. **Education examples**
   http://www.ucas.com   Universities and Colleges
       Admissions Service

3. **Abbreviation example**
   http://www.aprs.co.uk   Association of Professional
       Recording Services

Note: **Occasionally** you may wish to extend your research outside the UK so address endings such as fr (France) ca (Canada) nz (New Zealand) au (Australia) and us (United States) may well yield good results.

> **Useful Tips:** On discovering the sites of real interest, it is a very good idea to **Bookmark/Add to Favourites**. Your choices can then be viewed more quickly on your return.

Search Engines
There are occasions when guesswork, searches offered by ISPs and even some web sites, just don't come up with the goods. It may be then that

you want to call up the services of search engines, which are designed to interrogate masses of directories; quite amazingly in just split seconds. By far the front runner, and voted the most popular in a recent online survey by the *Financial Times* (ft.com) was Google. However, your particular information need may suggest using alternatives as briefly outlined below:

www.google.co.uk – superb at word searching
www.ask.co.uk – can write question in full. Also excellent for e-commerce

> **Useful Tips:** While ISP's own search box can be helpful, search engines are more likely to yield better results, particularly when using very specific words.

Finding the Information Gems

Let us assume you have located a particular site of interest and arrived at the colourful and usually informative Home Pages ready to explore its contents. As mentioned above, when explaining the star-rated evaluation of existing sites, there are particular details to look out for when researching careers information. The bad news, as one might expect with the Internet, being totally unregulated, is that organisations and particularly professional associations often locate or title their material into internal familiar names. However, the good news is that in the research of this publication, I was fortunate enough to identify a wide range of words or phrases, which I hope will encourage you to more easily identify those otherwise elusive gems.

Examples of commonly used key words and phrases

> **Careers   Jobs   Employment   Recruitment**
> **Personnel   Case studies   Profiles   Human resources**

All these titles are interchangeable and often used for giving information about the career. There is some overlap in this area, as the very same titles can refer to job opportunities, more usually listed as **Vacancies**. Other keywords/phrases include:

Education   Training   Continuing Professional Development (CPD)

Having now convinced yourself that your career interest warrants closer research, the next natural step is to find all you need on how to get into the profession: the entry requirements such as qualifications or professional experience, as well as opportunities for further education and training. Again, do not be surprised to find the details you are looking for within seemingly unrelated titles.

Frequently Asked Questions (FAQs)

This topic deserves special mention, as the Internet has greatly encouraged this creative approach to giving the public, as well as potential employees in this case, easy access to inside information. You can pick up brilliant detail, which can help you ask more perceptive questions at interview, as well as get a better idea of what working for a particular organisation might really be like!

Links and Related Sites

It can be very disappointing when a professional organisation has little or no careers information. However, do not despair, as Links are a common feature of web sites and are often an exciting source of further research you can usually explore from the Home Pages. Within seconds you could be directed to a related site down the road, or anywhere in the world. It is also an excellent research tool for students.

Journals and Publications

You will not want to miss this if you are really keen on a particular profession. It is a great way of keeping in touch with all the issues. Some journals can be accessed completely free. Others may be included with your professional membership of an organisation and if you are studying it is worth checking whether there are any special rates for students. At some stage you are likely to need a personal number to access the site. However, many journals can be 'sampled' for free, and often include back copies of previous editions, which can be great for research. Look out for archive pages.

Site Map

If you are ever stuck, as I was occasionally when researching the finer details for this book, then seek out the **site map**. Most organisations include this title within the Home Pages, and it is often the quickest way to locate particular information needs. If not clearly indicated in the home page contents listing, do scroll/page down the screen as it is not unusual to see the site map at the foot of the page.

About Us

This is quite a common and useful title and is usually listed on the index column of the home page. However, many organisations take this opportunity to introduce themselves, as well as mention valuable labour market information. This might include how many staff work in the company and new employment trends and targets. Also check out the news pages as this can also include similar content.

Useful Tips: Occasionally if you are within a site and no titles seem to relate to what you are looking for, try the site's own search facility.

Other Sources of Help

When it comes to accessing up-to-date careers and educational information, one of the best kept secrets, sadly, is the local Careers Centre. Most have excellent resources, and in particular, the larger offices should have comprehensive information systems which include:

- Careers leaflets from professional bodies and organisations.
- College and university prospectuses.
- Careers books.
- Careers and education directories.
- Computer software programs (including increasingly Internet access).
- Careers and education videos.

All resources are classified, as are the main references in this book, by CLCI (see below), so if in the final analysis the Internet has let you down, there is still much help freely available and it is an excellent way of connecting to other related services.

Note: Careers Library Classification Index

I wish to acknowledge and thank the Department for Education and Skills (DfES) for the opportunity to structure web sites within the national Careers Library Classification Index (CLCI). The CLCI uniquely brings together education, employment and training information with complementary careers, guidance, health and general reference sources.

For the purposes of this book only, and for convenience, some artistic licence has been necessary to reduce what are eighteen major job categories into six occupational groupings (see Contents). Two such examples include placing care for animals within a broader health category, and placing armed forces careers within the chapter on law, security and protection services.

Part One

Careers

1
Administration, Business and Management

If you are the type of person that thrives on challenges within a constantly changing environment, then perhaps a career in administration, business and management is for you. Society cannot function without organisations, and organisations, however large or small, cannot be effective without the right people in place. The wheels of national and local government alone employ in the region of three million staff in a great variety of roles. Likewise the NHS which, apart from its medical professionals (see Chapter 3), has the challenge of managing a huge business of £46 billion, in England alone, as a public service. Our industrial and commercial businesses are the lifeblood of a successful economy with their goods and services at home and abroad, providing valuable finances to the Exchequer as well as tremendous opportunities for employment. We are also in the midst of a dynamic IT revolution, constantly developing and significantly impacting on all our lives. Every sector of business and administration is applying IT to store, process, retrieve and present its information. As we embark on the twenty-first century, it has been suggested that over half of the UK's workforce already directly use IT in their jobs, compared with one in four just three years ago. Who would have predicted the enormous growth in employment opportunities such as careers associated with web site development, mobile communications and electronic entertainment systems? It is only a matter of time before we see the benefits of networked flat-screen web TVs in our homes that all the family can use for tasks ranging from learning and training, to entertainment and on-line shopping, for just about all our material needs.

Skills and Interests
There are a number of key skills and personal qualities in the world of business and commerce, but here are a few ideas which may encourage you to research further:

- Enjoy working with people and getting the best out of them.

- Meeting deadlines, running projects and administering budgets.

- Following systems and procedures with particular attention to detail.

- Assisting with correspondence, keeping records and making appointments.

- Making sure resources are used in the most effective way.

- Implementing policy initiated by government or an organisation.

- High level of information technology knowledge.

- Good communication and interpersonal skills.

Organisations and Work Environment
Civil service, European Union, local government, health and public services, commercial & industrial companies, human resource consultancies, IT industry, business and management services.

By their very nature, businesses are extremely diverse, requiring a broad range of skills. There are opportunities ranging from self-employment to working for large multinational concerns. Many careers within this sector are interchangeable, except where specific professional qualifications may be required.

The Jobs
Almost too numerous to mention for the larger concerns, and most of the specialist careers are also covered in other more appropriate sections of this book. However, the backbone to any successful organisation, whether large or small, may include any number of the following staff:

Receptionist	Administrative Assistant	Secretary
Junior Manager	Administrative Officer	Accountant
Librarian	Bilingual Linguist	Personnel Manager
Departmental Manager	Information Manager	Health Practice Manager
Lawyer	Diplomat	Farm Secretary
Bursar	Chartered Secretary	Researcher
Business Analyst	Network Manager	Computer Analyst
Programmer	Computer Engineer	Software Engineer
Operations Manager	Systems Designer	Computer/IT Consultant
Web Manager	Data Processing Operator	Multimedia Programmer
Local Government Officer	Software Trainer	Database Administrator
Tax Inspector	Trade Union Official	Health Service Administrator

CIVIL SERVICE, EUROPEAN UNION AND LOCAL GOVERNMENT
CLCI CODES: C–CAG

This is a great careers area to begin with, as the Internet has 'flung the doors open' to access government information. Most government agencies (see also general information sources in the Appendix) and departments have their own web sites which include information on recruitment. Access is made all the easier with a new portal at **ukonline.gov.uk** and links to over a thousand Internet sites. Should you get beyond the first application hurdles and want to impress at interview, then do check out the press release pages of the Central Office of Information at **coi.gov.uk** for all the latest topical information. If interested or, better still, confident in the use of other languages, then Europe could well be the launch pad to your international career. European Institutions can be located at **europa.eu.int** but you will need to check out individual sites to see if there is any worthy careers information. However, the recruitment pages from the European Commission's London site at **cec.org.uk** may be more helpful with current vacancies and brief, but useful, background information. Local Government careers are well represented below, but do also drop into complementary sites at **lg-employers.gov.uk**, **idea.gov.uk** and **lgcnet.com**

British Council   britcoun.org

A real eye-opener to the impressive work of the British Council which operates in 110 countries worldwide. If seeking employment on the global stage, drop into working with us and job vacancies for all the help you need. There is also a useful CV guide and application form on-line.

★★   (CLCI: CAB)

Chartered Institution of Taxation   tax.org.uk

If you have an interest in figures and finance then visit the students of tax pages for links to excellent careers information, prospectus details and information on Exam Training. For those taking elements of tax within their course of study at university, there is even advice on what specific reference books to look out for! However, if higher education is not for you, the site also complements entry to the Association of Taxation Technicians. The ATT site at **att.org.uk** includes advice about the range of trainee and professional routes into the industry as well as useful case studies of individuals working with tax.

★★★ (CLCI: CAB)

Civil Service civil-service.gov.uk

This Civil Service Gateway is hugely helpful for anyone considering a career in any one of the government departments. Whether a school or college leaver, graduate or career changer with specialist skills, you should find something of interest. There is also information on work experience and an opportunity to explore current vacancies in different regions of the country. The Fast Stream Development Programme is designed for high calibre graduates being groomed as potential leaders of tomorrow. If this more academic route appeals, then go straight to the dedicated site at **faststreamgov.uk**

★★★ (CLCI: CAB)

Customs and Excise hmce.gov.uk

Look into site map and step into the future pages for the real gems. This site provides a useful link to the recruitment offices around the UK. Customs and Excise employ in the region of 23,000 people at various grades. Whilst the fight against drug trafficking and other illegal trade is one of the highest priorities and attracting wide media interest; collecting Value Added Tax and regulating Excise and Inland Customs are still vital areas of work.

★★ (CLCI: CAB)

Foreign and Commonwealth Office fco.gov.uk

Whether you're a student of politics, interested in foreign affairs or considering a career in the Foreign and Commonwealth Office, this award-winning web site is well worth visiting. It has everything from news archive material, key foreign policy issues and speeches, to the latest government travel advice. There is a wealth of information on recruitment, selection and entry procedures. The FCO also flies the flag for equal opportunities.

★★★ (CLCI: CAB)

Government Communications Headquarters gchq.gov.uk

You would think this site was designed specifically for potential employees. The nature of working in government communications is confidentiality, so what this site may lack in public information is more than made up for in careers information. There are excellent details on clerical, administrative and technical opportunities at GCHQ, as well as student sponsorship, graduate management training schemes and specialist professions. New features to this site include vacancy listings and career profiles.

★★★ (CLCI: CAB)

Local Government **lgnto.gov.uk**

Those unfamiliar with the workings of local government may be surprised that it can represent over 500 different occupations. Students and job seekers will appreciate the careers links to **lgcareers.com** and careers community pages of this site. Excellent images help you explore a range of essential services. See also the routes into local government for education and training information. The jobs section at **lgjobs.com** encourages you to search by county or occupational group, but don't miss the potential research opportunities and check out the list of employers. On offer is a direct link to district and borough council web sites.

★★★ (CLCI: CAG)

UK Public Sector Information **ukonline.gov.uk**

You could spend hours here, particularly if you stumble across the official web site of the monarchy, the on-line journal 'Royal Insight' and much more. However, this site is packed with other links to over 1,000 government sites and a number of useful indexes, to help you find what you are looking for.

★★★ (CLCI: CAB)

Other Sites of Interest

10 Downing Street	**number-10.gov.uk**
Cabinet Office	**cabinet-office.gov.uk**
CAPITA RAS	**rasnet.co.uk**
Convention of Scottish Local Authorities	**cosla.gov.uk**
European Union On-line	**europe.eu.int**
HM Customs and Excise	**hmce.gov.uk**
Local Government	**lg.gov.uk**
Local Government Association	**lga.gov.uk**
Local Government Vacancies	**lgjobs.com**

Local Government Vacancies	**datalake.com/lgo**
The Northern Ireland Office	**nio.gov.uk**
Scottish Executive	**scotland.gov.uk**
Scottish Parliament	**scottish.parliament.uk**
Treasury Office	**hm-treasury.gov.uk**
UK Local Government Information	**brent.gov.uk/other/uk-locl.htm**
The National Assembly for Wales	**wales.gov.uk**

HEALTH, PUBLIC SERVICE AND BUSINESS MANAGEMENT ADMIN, PERSONNEL AND SECRETARIAL
CLCI CODES: CAL-CAT

There are fewer highly rated sites in this sector, but many include interesting features, such as access to specific trade journals and details on specialist qualifications such as professional administration. In addition, you will notice that organisations are including specific training courses for staff and news of forthcoming events and conferences. The Internet is a great way to keep up to date with your own professional organisation, as well as gaining excellent insights that can help your confidence at interview, and leave a very good impression with prospective employers. If still in school or college and wanting to seize opportunities to encourage your enterprising potential then **young-enterprise.org.uk** is certainly worth noting. You could then launch your career in business with **leaders-of-tomorrow.co.uk**! The success of any organisation is often due to good administrators, so drop into **cfa.uk.com** to see what type of training is possible.

Business and Economics on the Internet   bized.ac.uk

This is a brilliant resource for sixth-form or undergraduate students studying business or economics. You can browse an extensive Business Internet catalogue, and link to the FTSE 100 top companies in the UK and their web sites, which you can use to seek out opportunities for employment. You can even download virtual company and economy packages to help with projects. Do check the What's New pages for useful tips on study skills and types of exam questions.
★★   (CLCI: CAP)

Business on the Internet   bnet.co.uk

Short on careers information, but a wealth of business-related gems for the serious student or business manager. The subscribing Links pages look particularly noteworthy, but do first check the free Links Archives.

★★ (CLCI: CAP)

Health Service Journal — **hsj.co.uk**

This is a must for the serious health professional. Once beyond the registration phase you can tap into a valuable source of information. There is an excellent Jobs Plus service, featured articles, health gossip and book reviews. Also a specific search engine for locating academic and clinical health care professionals.

★★ (CLCI: CAL)

Institute of Personnel and Development — **ipd.co.uk**

Drop into Careers for detail on the work of pesonnel and development professionals, gaining experience, salaries, personal characteristics and qualifications. The site also links you to People Management, the IPD's professional journal, but you will need to be a member to access the specialist job-hunting site.

★★★ (CLCL: CAS)

National Health Service Management — **nhs-mtsandmesol.demon.co.uk**

This is a very useful site to visit if you are an aspiring Health Service Manager, or already in post and looking for professional development through open learning. You will find all the details you require on entering such a career, as well as useful work profiles of different managers. The Management Scheme for Open Learning (Mesol) can advise individuals or organisations on opportunities for further health and social care training with support from centres across the UK.

★★ (CLCI: CAL)

Post Office — **ukpo.com**

The Post Office is now officially a public company, so this site provides a good opportunity to keep in touch with new initiatives, as well as familiar services.

★ (CLCI: CAM)

PricewaterhouseCoopers **pwcglobal.com/uk**

PricewaterhouseCoopers are among the country's leading management consultants. This is a great site for keeping in touch with the world of international business and finance. There are also very good pages for graduates or undergraduates on anything from summer vacation placements to gap year, work shadowing and current employment opportunities.

★★ (CLCI: CAP)

The Times 1000 **the times100.co.uk**

Business Studies students and teachers will be particularly inspired by this excellent site, which offers a helpful search by subject and comprehensive case study resource. Also, don't miss the complementary careers file section and Focus on Career Fields in particular. You will be spoilt with really useful information on a broad range of jobs, as well as appropriate hot-links to many professional assocations.

★★★ (CLCI:CAP)

Other Sites of Interest

Association of British Recovery Professionals	**insolvency.org.uk**
British Chamber of Commerce	**britishchambers.org.uk**
British Employment Law	**emplaw.co.uk**
British Quality Foundation	**quality-foundation.co.uk**
Business & Training Information	**thebiz.co.uk**
Business Finder	**scoot2.co.uk**
Business Management Information	**bnet.co.uk**
CAPITA RAS	**rasnet.co.uk**
Centre for Public Services	**centre.public.co.uk**
Companies House	**companies-house.gov.uk**
Confederation of British Industry	**cbi.org.uk**
Corporate Social Responsibility Forum	**csrforum.com**
The Council for Administration	**cfa.uk.com**
European Business Directory	**europages.com**
European Industrial Relations	**eiro.eurofound.ie**
Federation of Small Businesses	**fsb.org.uk**
Institute of Administrative Management	**instam.org**
Institute of Chartered Secretaries and Administrators	**icsa.org.uk**
Institute of Global Communications	**igc.org**
Institute of Health Care Management	**ihm.co.uk**

Institute of Personnel and Development	**ipd.co.uk**
Institute of Qualified Private Secretaries	**iqps.org**
International Association of Bookkeepers	**accountingweb.org.uk**
International Christian Chamber of Commerce	**uk.iccc.net**
International Personnel Management Association	**ipma-hr.org**
Leaders of Tomorrow	**leaders-of-tomorrow.co.uk**
Management Resource	**theantidote.co.uk**
NHS Executive	**doh.gov.uk/nhs.htm**
NHS Management Scheme	**mts.nhs.uk**
Northern Ireland Public Service Union	**nipsa.org.uk**
Office Angels Recruitment	**office-angels.com**
Online Training	**etrain.com**
People Management	**peoplemanagement.co.uk**
Small Business Advice Service	**smallbusinessadvice.org.uk**
Small Business Bureau	**businessbureau-uk.co.uk**
Small Business Service	**businesslink.org**
SME Business Information	**bird-online.co.uk**
Supplier of Business Opportunity and Info Factsheet series	**cobwebinfo.com**
The Times 1000	**thetimes100.co.uk**
Trade Union Congress	**tuc.org.uk**
UK Online for Business	**ukonlineforbusiness.gov.uk**
UNICEF	**unicef.org.uk**
Unison	**unison.org.uk**
STEP Graduate Recruitment	**step.org.uk**
Young Enterprise	**young-enterprise.org.uk**

INFORMATION TECHNOLOGY
CLCI CODE: CAV

Perhaps the bubble will burst one day, when technological innovation begins to occupy the very same jobs it helped to create. However, until then and with current demand for web managers and designers, there is much to be encouraged about. The profession is teeming with sites eager to set you off in the right direction, including choosing university courses with **whichuni.hobsons.com** and **ucas.com**. There are also excellent current vacancy lists from sites such as **computerweekly.co.uk** and **jobscout.co.uk**. If you are searching specifically from your IT experience then also check out **computerstaff.net** and others listed towards the end of this section. Many sites such as **vnunet.com** and **cssa.co.uk** will help you keep pace with the very latest IT developments.

British Computer Society   **bcs.org.uk**

I must commend the 'Continuing Professional Development' entries that form part of accredited courses with BCS. There is also a wealth of useful information for young people and teachers within the schools student & YPG and Education pages. The pages included such gems as help on making those all important choices for higher education. There is excellent careers information as well as the much acclaimed 'Survival Kits for Jobhunters'.

★★★   (CLCI: CAY)

E-Skills   **e-skills.com**

Useful site for anyone considering a career in IT. The IT Compass Section looks to be particularly informative about one exciting opportunity in this fast-moving industry. There is helpful vocational information and excellent link pages.

★★   (CLCI: CAV)

Institute for the Management of Information Systems   **imis.org.uk**

It is claimed that 20 per cent of what we know about information technology becomes obsolete each year and therefore investment in training and development of staff is essential to the success of any business. This site has a useful facility to download pdf files on Careers in Information Systems and links to opportunities for young people and MBA mentoring.

★   (CLCI: CAV)

Women in Science, Engineering and Technology   **set4women.gov.uk**

Women currently make up less than 15 per cent of the full time industrial and academic workforce in Science, Engineering and Technology (SET). This site tackles the challenge to encourage the young graduates as well as potential returners, to look afresh at the amazing opportunities for women in SET. The schools pages include useful information for teachers, excellent 'role model' job profiles and access to the Spark magazine designed for 14–16 year old girls.

Other Sites of Interest
The Ability Project   **ability.org.uk**
British Educational Communications

& Technology Agency	**becta.org.uk**
British Interactive Multimedia Association	**bima.co.uk**
Computer Books	**ineasysteps.com**
Computer Staff	**computerstaff.net**
Computers Don't Bite	**bbc.co.uk/education/cdb**
Computing Services and Software Association	**cssa.co.uk**
E-Business	**silicon.com**
Education and the Internet	**ultralab.anglia.ac.uk**
Electronics and Software Recruitment	**e-and-s-recruitment.co.uk**
European Association of Computer Graphics	**eg.org**
IBM	**ibm.com**
Institute of IT Training	**iitt.org.uk**
IT Contractor Portal	**contractoruk.co.uk**
IT Job Link	**itjoblink.com**
IT Job Seek	**itjobseek.co.uk**
IT Opportunities	**4weeks.com**
Job Scout	**jobscout.co.uk**
Microsoft Vacancies	**microsoft.com/jobs**
National Computing Centre	**ncc.co.uk**
Recruitlink	**recruitlink.co.uk**
Shop Creator	**shopcreator.com**
UK Technology News	**vnunet.com**

POLITICS, MANAGEMENT SERVICES, RESEARCH AND OCCUPATIONAL SAFETY
CLCI CODES: COB-COZ

Who would ever want to become a politician within our blame culture and sleaze-obsessed media? Yet, while core values and standards crumble all around us, one could argue that never before have we needed such a force of integrity to influence society for good. So, if you are interested in a career in politics, do not be put off by the lack of careers information on the Internet. You can still be encouraged by checking out your political party's web site. There may be little on what it might be like to 'work the local patch', by a counsellor or member of parliament, but if you want details on manifestos, how to e-mail your MP, or searching for political speeches, then you are sure to find something of interest. If you are politically keen on conservation issues, then the Green Party's site at **gn.apc.org** is well worth a visit, with links to over 200 associated organisations. Management services is well covered with some excellent sites, but strongly recommend is leafing back a few pages to Business Management for additional web sites. It is encouraging to see occupational and safety standard organisations such as **britishsafetycouncil.co.uk** and **bsi-global.com** now including careers information.

British Institute of Occupational Hygienists   **bioh.org**

Need to locate the Site Index and FAQ Index before reaching the informative details on Occupational Hygiene as a Career.

★   (CLCI COT)

The Chartered Institute of Environmental Health   **cieh.org.uk**

This has everything you need to know about how to train for a career in environmental health and further courses for continuing professional development, once established in the profession. There are also some interesting features and topics to research further.

★★★   (CLCI: COP)

The Ergonomics Society   **ergonomics.org.uk**

You need to go into Ergonomics to discover just what this fascinating concept of fitting design around people and efficiency is all about.. The education pages help you appreciate what it will be like to study such a specialist subject, as well as offer links to all the approved courses in the UK. There are also details on four current Human Factors and Psychology courses that are particularly well suited for graduates wanting to become Associate Members. The jobs section includes current vacancies, as well as short-term work placements and the links read like a who's who in the international world of ergonomics and human factors (USA).

★★★   (CLCI: COD)

Greenpeace International   greenpeace.org

This site has to be rated, just for the sheer volume of amazing data. Every kind of topical as well as lesser-known environmental issues are explored. You can also use their extensive web links to locate further gems. The political arm can be located at **gn.apc.org**.

★   (CLCI: COB)

Institute for the Management of Information Systems   **imis.org.uk**

It is claimed that 20 per cent of what we know about information technology becomes obsolete each year and therefore investment in training and development of staff is essential to the success of any business. This site has a useful facility to download pdf files on Careers in Information Systems and links to opportunities for young people and MBA mentoring.

★ (CLCI: COD)

Institute of Management   **inst-mgt.org.uk**

If you're planning a career in management, then check out the Career Development, Guidelines and Careers in Management Factsheet pages. There is excellent advice on job-searching, writing a CV and even choosing a second career. There is even help if you are feeling stressed in business, perhaps having experienced downsizing or just far too many changes. The site is highly rated for much more, including Management Links, which will connect you with other professional related web sites. If that is not enough, then there is the on-line IM bookstore you can order from, but which is also an excellent reference tool on management publications. Members of the Institute have access to further counselling and career development information, as well as use of the Legal Helpline and Outplacement Counselling Services.

★★★ (CLCI: COD)

Institute of Management Consultancy   **imc.co.uk**

The Careers section of this site looks very useful and includes education (up to Master's Degree), training and recruitment information. If you are already in a business and considering using management consultants to help you implement important changes, then check out Consultants pages for some excellent preparatory tips. News links you to Europe's latest business headlines, but don't miss Our Web Library for some great features and articles.

★★ (CLCI: COD)

Institution of Occupational Safety and Health   **iosh.co.uk**

ISOH is Europe's leading body for individuals with a professional involvement in occupational safety and health. The site includes brief but useful careers information and university and open learning details within Professional Development. For wider research be encouraged by dropping into the impressive links pages.

★★ (CLCI: COT)

Management Consultants Association   **mca.org.uk**

This site provides access to many of the biggest names in management consultancy. On registering you can explore company sites in more detail, check out their career openings or perhaps develop your own ideas to run a management consultancy. The careers information pages include personal profiles of people entering the profession. As well as locating companies in your region, there is the chance to check if any of the firms have taken on recent graduates, run vacation work schemes, or have current vacancies. The site includes useful links to related organisations in the UK and overseas.

★★   (CLCI: COD)

Operational Research Society   **orsoc.org.uk**

From 'Quick Find and Careers in OR' you can access the full text of the society's excellent careers publication *Careers in Operational Research*. This includes likely future employment opportunities, professional development and postgraduate course information. There is also a free interactive multimedia programme designed for schools introducing OR as a career. The profiles are also great for getting a real feel for what OR work is really like, and if looking for work then you don't have to look far with banner ads splashing the top of your screen! This is also a great site if you are a potential student. You can check out the Learning Aids pages to see how particular case studies and methodologies are used in OR assignments. Within Study Groups you will come across a wide range of current projects and the teams leading them. There are also interesting links to other European and international societies.

★★★   (CLCI: COF)

Political Studies Association   **psa.ac.uk**

You will not be disappointed with this web site, as it has a real international presence. There are also opportunities to order on-line study or political interest resources. However, one of the key features is the impressive Web Gateway and links to over 4,000 related sites, as well as a graduate network and postgraduate discussion clubs. If that is not enough, try out the research sources at Libraries and Archives or see what **politicalstudies.org** has to offer.

★★   (CLCI: COB)

Other Sites of Interest

British Institute of Occupational Hygienists	**bioh.org**
British Occupational Hygiene Society	**bohs.org**
British Safety Council	**britishsafetycouncil.co.uk**
British Standards Institute	**bsi-global.com**
Business Directory	**yell.co.uk**
Chartered Institute of Environmental Health	**cieh.org.uk**
Christian Peoples Alliance	**cpalliance.net**
Computing Services and Software Association	**cssa.co.uk**
Conservative Party	**conservative.com**
Consultants News (USA)	**kennedypub.com/cn**
Corporate Training Services	**careers-training.com**
Electoral Commission	**party-register.gov.uk**
European Parliament	**europarl.eu.int**
European Agency for Safety & Health at Work	**http://europe.osha.eu.int/**
Euroqual	**euroqual.org**
Executive & Senior Management Courses	**managementcourses.com**
Green Party of England and Wales	**gn.apc.org**
Health and Safety Executive	**hse.gov.uk**
Health, Environment and Work – University of Edinburgh	**med.ed.ac.uk/hew**
House of Commons	**parliament.uk**
Institute of Management Services	**dircon.co.uk/imgtserv**
Institute of Quality Assurance	**iqa.org**
The Institution of Occupational Safety and Health	**iosh.co.uk**
International Organisation for Standardisation	**iso.ch/welcome.html**
Kelly's Directory	**kellys.co.uk**
Kompass Directory	**kompass.com**
The Labour Party	**labour.org.uk**
Liberal Democrats	**libdems.org.uk**
Management and Enterprise Training Organisation	**meto.org.uk**
Office of Fair Trading	**oft.gov.uk**
Plaid Cymru	**plaidcymru.org**
The Royal Institute of Public Health and Hygiene	**riphh.org.uk**
Scottish National Party	**snp.org.uk**
The Society of Food Hygiene Technology	**sofht.co.uk**
Ulster Democratic Unionist Party	**dup.org.uk**
Ulster Unionist Party	**uup.org**
Video Arts	**videoarts.co.uk**
White House (USA)	**whitehouse.gov**

2
Creative, Cultural and Leisure

Everything around us has to be designed before it can be made. You only have to look about your home or workplace, while travelling or pursuing leisure interests, to see creativity at play. It may shout from the media through advertising, commercial radio or television. On other occasions it may perhaps appear more subtly, for example when coming across a beautiful landscape, being totally absorbed in a good book, or wearing comfortable clothes. The combined influence of the arts and information technology is keenly felt in this diverse sector with increased access to the Internet and digital technology. This is resulting in an information revolution that will increasingly interface with careers in art and design, education and publishing, as well as related occupations in the entertainment, sport and leisure industries. Increasingly our businesses recognise the importance of design as a strategic asset in order to succeed in world markets. No doubt our young people, stimulated much earlier by the invitation to the creative feast, will open up new opportunities for the next generation. The exciting challenge for anyone entering or redefining their place in such careers is discovering just what their natural gifts are and then using every opportunity to develop and perhaps release the as yet untapped resources within.

Skills and Interests
Listed below are a range of interests and abilities that are used in the creative, cultural and leisure industries. Some may be very specific to art-related careers, but others can be applied across a range of jobs.

- Enjoy free expression, artistic and imaginative and can visualise end results.

- Eye for tone and colour and prepared to accept criticism and rejection of ideas.

- Prepared to take risks in highly competitive situations.

- Methodical, pay attention to detail and accurate.

- Practical, innovative and resourceful.

- Self-motivated and prepared if necessary to be self-employed.

- Understand technical processes and IT literate.

- High levels of commitment and can keep to deadlines.

- Build trusting relationships with children, parents and colleagues.

- Inspired by the use of languages, different cultures and travel.

- Desire to enthuse others with your specialist knowledge and gifts.

- Physically fit and healthy.

- Gain much satisfaction in providing high quality service.

Organisations and Work Environments

Public services, multimedia firms, private businesses, multinational companies, government bodies, design, photographic and musical studios, education establishments and institutions, local authorities, national, regional and local media and broadcasting organisations, research departments, theatrical companies, sport and health clubs, outdoor pursuit and leisure centres, holiday resorts and tourism agencies, entertainment centres and theme parks.

The Jobs – Creative

Artist	Graphic Designer	Illustrator
Industrial and Craft Designer	Textile Designer	Photographer
Fashion Buyer	Textile Technician	Model Maker
Photographic Technician	Fashion Designer	Web Designer
Advertising and Marketing	Signwriter	Art Director
Interior Design and Display	Potter	Architect
Stonemason	Cartoonist	Animator

Note: There are careers associated with this sector but related more to science and technology, such as printmaking, design, product engineering and technical illustration plus others related to the environment and land services such as architecture or landscape architecture (Chapter 6).

GRAPHIC ART AND DESIGN, ILLUSTRATION AND CRAFT DESIGN
CLCI CODES: E–EG

The Internet provides a great opportunity to visit exhibitions on-line, inspire your particular interests and abilities, as well as keep you right up to date with education and career developments. Good examples can be found at **netgain.org.uk** and **metier.org.uk** which provide information and guidance on the arts. If you are in business and looking for consultants or trainers in the arts, then why not check out **arts-consultants.org.uk**. Web design is covered within CAV.

Artists Information Company   artistscareers.co.uk

This site is dedicated to supporting visual artists throughout their professional life. It asks crucial questions like 'What is it like to be an artist?', 'Will I be on the dole forever?' and 'How can I earn a living as an artist?' Check the What kinds of jobs are out there section for useful personal insights from folk who have 'worn the T-shirt'.
★★   (CLCI: ED)

Arts Council of England   artscouncil.org.uk

See Jobs for any current vacancies in the Council itself, but the site also has some particularly good links to community arts and festival pages, all regional art boards and news information. The Directory pages are packed with details on art funding.
★★   (CLCI: E)

Design Council   design-council.org.uk

Recent available research showed that the value of design to the UK economy was some £12 billion, with 300,000 people employed in the field. You could spend hours at this site researching design concepts that have worked. Check Design Information and directory pages within Design Horizons for amazing A–Z of contact organisations.
★   (CLCI: ED)

European Links to Arts, Entertainment   eurochannel.de/
and Leisure Sites

Unlikely to find much careers information here, but a very good site if researching European information in almost any of the arts.

★ (CLCI: E/F/G/I)

Institute of Medical Illustrators   imi.org.uk

If you would like the challenge of working precisely to record medical conditions whilst also using flair and initiative to help others visualise your ideas, then you have come to the right place. This site has useful careers, education and links pages to research.

★★ (CLCI: ED)

Online Regional Arts Pages   arts.org.uk

Become immersed in this excellent site, which I just could not rate highly enough. Whether you are at an early stage in your career ideas, thinking seriously about courses to encourage your creative interest or using your skills to find work, you will get great advice here. The site is also designed (text-only browser) to help the visually impaired locate the same information. You can search on all the main art disciplines, from dance to craft as well as further web and e-mail links. Locating detail within specific regions is painless, and the training pages will help you research the right courses including part-time, further and higher education. There is excellent advice on funding, and the business pages will be a great encouragement to those preferring or having to be self-employed.

★★★ (CLCI: E)

Open College of the Arts   oca-uk.com

This site is ideally suited to self-motivated individuals who would rather work at their own pace from home than follow a course at a school or college. OCA works on the principle that everyone has artisitic ability. Their aim is to help you to both discover and reach your full creative potential.

★★ (CLCI: E)

The Stage Weekly Journal   thestage.co.uk

The Auditions and Recruitment pages will keep you well informed on a wide range of creative jobs, from work in the theatre to holiday club compères and writing for TV & radio.

★ (CLCI: E)

UK Theatre Web   uktw.co.uk

Some useful information on jobs and training, particularly for technicians and stage managers, who can also submit their CV by e-mail for potential vacancies. However, this is a great site if you wish to explore the whole area of performing arts. There are links to the lesser-known skills of clowning and to the UK Actors Directory and the major film distributors' web sites. See also G-GAF.

★★   (CLCI: E)

Other Sites of Interest

Arts Information Network	**netgain.org.uk**
Association of Illustrators	**aoi.co.uk**
British Art	**britart.com**
British Artist Blacksmiths' Association	**baba.org.uk**
British Jewellers Association	**bja.org.uk**
Chartered Society of Designers	**csd.org.uk**
Craft Council (USA)	**craftcouncil.org**
Crafts Council	**craftscouncil.org.uk**
European Association for Computer Graphics	**eg.org**
Fine Art Search Engine	**artcyclopedia.com**
Industrial Design International	**icsid.org**
Institute of Packaging	**iop.co.uk**
Institute of Scientific and Technical Communicators	**istc.org.uk**
Institution of Engineering Designers	**ied.org.uk**
National Association of Goldsmiths	**progold.net**
Register of Consultants and Trainers in the Arts	**arts-consultants.org.uk**
Royal Academy of Arts	**royalacademy.org.uk**
Royal College of Art	**rca.ac.uk**

FASHION AND INTERIOR DESIGN, DISPLAY AND PHOTOGRAPHY
CLCI CODES: EJ–EZ

British fashion designers enjoy a very successful international reputation! Youth culture demands fresh and vibrant ideas and so being flexible and open to constant change is important. What better way to keep up to date than checking out the latest fashion such as can be found at **fashionweb.co.uk** and **firstview.com/designerlist**. They may be short on careers information, so don't miss others listed below. Meanwhile the IT industry is revolutionising the demands in photography with the need for instant electronic imaging to enhance and manipulate photographs. Again, keep in touch with **rps.org** and other sites listed.

Association of Photographers   **aophoto.co.uk**

Check out Services for information on current vacancies. If you are thinking of going freelance, this is a great site to let people know of your particular professional skills. A good site too for keeping in touch with the industry and, particularly for the links to other web sites.

★   (CLCI: EV)

British Institute of Professional Photography   **bipp.com**

If you are looking for an on-line guide to a career in photography then look no further than the Student and Assistants pages. This is also a great site for the seasoned professional who may want to promote their business, or perhaps take advantage of many new training opportunities.

★★   (CLCI: EV)

CAPITB Trust   **careers-in-clothing.co.uk**

This is a terrific site to check out a range of careers opportunities associated with fashion and clothing. The careers and training pages are a great place to start with help on the many different education and training routes into the industry. There are career details within the Career Paths pages and Designer Fact File is there to guide the trained fashion designers.

★★★   (CLCI: EJ)

Interior Decorators and Designers Association   **idda.co.uk**

Helpful tips on what to look out for when choosing good courses in interior design. Visit the interior design and decoration village pages to get a real feel for the industry, but unfortunately this site has no careers information – yet!

★   (CLCI: ET)

Photo Imaging   **photoimaging.org**

The photographic industry in the UK employs over 48,000 people in some 7,000 companies. This site explores the many different career routes including processing, digital imaging and photography. There are useful college case studies and encouraging learn direct opportunities.

★★   (CLCI: EV)

Society of British Theatre Designers   **theatredesign.org.uk**

This is the site to come to for those wishing to get a feel for a career in theatre design. The gallery pages offer a series of stage designs which you can enlarge, together with brief production details. The course information is good and includes related areas such as theatre costume, make-up, sound and lighting. The links pages take you to some very useful further points of discovery.

★   (CLCI: ET)

Vogue   **vogue.co.uk**

If you are into the world of fashion and beauty you will just love this site and want to keep coming back. There are links to a number of fashion houses, catwalk reports and daily news from the fashion industry. The jobs in fashion pages are particularly impressive. You can search on business, marketing and PR, buying and merchandising, design, hair and beauty and others to find out what vacancies are out there, although the great majority are in London.

★★   (CLCI: EJ)

Zoom   **zoom.co.uk**

Zoom is an Internet Server with an interest in fashion. By searching on jobs you can enter the Arcadia Group pages which include school-leaver, college and graduate information. Arcadia is one of Europe's largest fashion retailers and offers an on-line graduate application form and an interactive assessment service.

★   (CLCI: EJ)

Other Sites of Interest

Art and Artefact	**artefact.co.uk**
British Apparel and Textile Confederation	**batc.co.uk**
British Footwear Association	**britfoot.com**
British Institute of Professional Photography	**bipp.com**
British Journal of Photography	**bjphoto.co.uk**
Fashion Collections	**firstview.com/designerlist**
Fashion Net (USA)	**fashion.net**
Fashion Television	**fashiontelevision.com**
Fashion Web	**fashionweb.co.uk**
Approved Footwear and Textiles	**skillfast.uk**
Into Fashion	**intofashion.com**

London Institute of Fashion	**tinst.ac.uk**
Marks and Spencer	**marks-and-spencer.com**
Master Photographers Association	**mpauk.com**
Metier	**metier.org.uk**
National Council for the Training Journalists	**nctj.com**
National Museum of Photography	**nmsi.ac.uk/nmpf**
Recruitment Media	**recruitmedia.co.uk**
Royal Photographic Society	**rps.org**
Scottish Textiles	**scottish-textiles.co.uk**
World of Interiors	**worldofinteriors.co.uk**

The Jobs – Cultural

Archaeologist	Teacher	Publisher
Journalist	Writer	Museum Curator
Librarian	Pastor	Historian
Information Manager	Classroom Assistant	Interpreter
Training Officer	Information Scientist	Translator
Anthropologist	Archivist	Editor
Conservationist	Curator	Indexer
Lecturer	Nursery Teacher	Technical Author

TEACHING, JOURNALISM AND PUBLISHING
CLCI CODES: F–FAD

Arguably, teaching is one of the most talked about modern-day professions. Sadly though, it is often a political and media football being kicked and coerced around the latest topical playground. However, no one can argue about the professionalism and consistent personal commitment that teachers give, which sometimes supplements poor parenting. The web offers some excellent careers information for aspiring teachers. However, if you are interested in exploring the specialist and renowned Montessori teaching of younger children, then **montessori.co.uk** is well worth checking out. Also tempting on the international scene for teachers looking for a fresh challenge is **cfbt.com**. Temporary and permanent staff vacancies can be found at **timeplan.com** but check the other sites of interest listed below. Journalism has been described as 10 per cent inspiration, 90 per cent perspiration. You may need a little of the latter if you want to explore fully the gems within all the sites listed below, but if you are looking at broadcasting journalism then **itv.co.uk** will link you to all their regional companies. Publishing is well represented on the web, but check the interesting and varied career articles at **thebookseller.com**

BBC — bbc.co.uk/jobs

This is a highly rated site for anyone seeking a career in broadcasting including journalism, programme making, business support and management and much more. Job seekers and work experience applicants can check out the positions vacant pages if aged 15–18.

★★★ (CLCI: FAC)

Broadcast Journalism Training Council — bjtc.org.uk

All the encouragement you need on training to be a broadcast journalist is on this site. The FAQs are certainly worth a visit and there is plenty of course information and links to college sites for even more detail. There is even advice for course leaders and colleges considering starting courses.

★★ (CLCI: FAC)

Department for Education and Skills — dfes.gov.uk

There are many references in this book to the DfES's web site. If you are involved specifically in education, then this is certainly the place to go for all the latest government thinking, circulars and news. The site index and search facilities will help you locate particular material, but suggest other sites listed if you are looking for careers information.

★★ (CLCI: FAB)

General Teaching Council for Scotland — gtcs.org.uk

If you are considering a teaching career in Scotland then this site will more than help your initial research, particularly the links to other web sites on education and training in Scotland. it's packed with useful gems and if your interest lies in the early years you will love the virtual teachers centre, again located from the links pages.

★★ (CLCI: FAB)

Kevins Playroom — kevinsplayroom.co.uk

It is no wonder this award winning homework and curriculum portal is getting such rave reviews. You can explore any curriculum subject and are then taken to a wealth of useful related resources on the web. Brief summaries help you decide whether to pursue any given site further, so saving you going down too many blind web alleys. My kids often play the games section, and if looking to the future the site also includes links to colleges and universities as well as a useful translator facility from English to five European languages.

★★★ (CLCI: FAB)

National Council for the Training of Journalists   **nctj.com**

Perhaps you are wondering whether journalism is for you. Be encouraged, as you will get excellent help on this site, beginning with the qualities that newspaper editors are looking for. There is excellent course information and links to other related web sites. There is even a Hall of Fame which may just have your name on it one day!

★★ (CLCI: FAC)

The Newspaper Society   **newspapersoc.org.uk**

You may need some investigative skills to locate the careers information, but once into the NS Services and Training pages you will find some very good material. There is information for school and college leavers and links to all the essential sites for further help. This is a particularly good site for project work as there are masses of facts and figures, reports and research papers.

★★ (CLCI: FAC)

Periodical Publishers Association   **ppa.co.uk**

You are really in for a treat here as this highly creative site is designed to inspire and encourage people into this very competitive but rewarding career. From the site map and careers pages there is plenty of careers information, help in selecting the right course and ultimately finding work through one of several recommended agencies. To top it all, the A–Z of publishers will connect you with over 200 other magazines on-line!

★★★ (CLCI: FAD)

Publishers Association   **publishers.org.uk**

The advice pages on getting your material published are a potential writer's dream. Do be encouraged though that it is often original ideas and identifying future readers' needs that impress publishers, so don't be discouraged at the first hurdles. Should you want to pursue a job in this demanding but exciting industry, then visit the very good careers in publishing pages on this site, which include valuable course information.

★★ (CLCI: FAD)

Publishing Training Centre   **train4publishing.co.uk**

The Internet is opening up some exciting learning opportunities and publishing is not excluded. You can study in your own home and at your own pace with distance learning courses in proofreading, editing and copywriting. The centre also offers over 60 different skill-based courses, to meet the industry's needs. At the time of writing, the national training organisation for publishing was under development, but this site includes some useful NTO information.

★ (CLCI: FAD)

Reuters   **reuters.com/careers**

If you are looking for a career in international journalism, then you are in for a treat at this site! You can explore in some detail a number of personal professional profiles, which mention the challenges of getting first to the news stories that Reuters is renowned for. It is worth checking the graduate programme pages particularly, as they are packed with useful information including insights into Reuters' innovative response to the potential of the Internet in media and business.

★★★ (CLCI: FAC)

Society of Freelance Editors and Proofreaders   **sfep.demon.co.uk**

The training pages are useful, but the FAQs provide a particularly good introduction to this specialist career.

★ (CLCI: FAD)

Teacher Training Agency   **canteach.gov.uk**

What's teaching really like, how can I train and what opportunities are there once I've qualified? These are just the questions this site is designed to answer. There is also useful financial advice and the FAQ pages are well worth looking at as they also have an e-mail advice service for potential teachers as well as possible returners to the profession.

★★★ (CLCL: FAB)

Virtual Teachers Centre   **vtc.ngfl.gov.uk**

Likely to be of most interest to the practising teacher, but still a good site for getting a feel for the profession and the amazing wealth of resources that are now available through IT. It is also worth checking out some of the excellent links to other web sites. Primary teachers will be more impressed with **teachingideas.co.uk**.

★★   (CLCI: FAB)

Worldwide Newspapers, Magazines and TV Stations   **ecola.com**

This site should be entered, just for its amazing source of contacts in the media professions. A useful companion site for searching newspapers on-line in the UK and overseas is **thepaperboy.co.uk**.

★   (CLCI: FAC)

Other Sites of Interest

Association of Learned and Professional Society Publishers	**alpsp.org.uk**
Association of University Teachers	**aut.org.uk**
Academic Careers Vacancies	**academiccareers.com**
Appointments for Teachers	**aft.co.uk**
The Bookseller	**thebookseller.com**
British Educational Communications and Technology Agency	**becta.org.uk**
CfBT Education Services	**cfbt.com**
Channel 4	**channel4.com**
Chartered Institute of Journalists	**users.dircon.co.uk/_cioj**
Education Jobs	**education-jobs.co.uk**
Electronic Telegraph	**telegraph.co.uk**
English Language Teaching Vacancies	**ef.com**
Innovation in Education and Industry	**tcd.co.uk**
Institute for Learning and Teaching in Higher Education	**ilt.ac.uk**
ITV	**itv.co.uk**
Jobs in Education	**jobsin.co.uk/education**
Jobs Times Educational Supplement	**jobs.tes.co.uk**
The Media Exchange (Job Hunting)	**themediaexchange.co.uk**
Montessori Teaching	**montessori.co.uk/page24.htm**
National Association of Head Teachers	**naht.org.uk**
Press Association	**pa.press.net**
Primary Teaching Ideas	**teachingideas.co.uk**

Publishers Association	**publishers.org.uk**
Publishing Training Centre	**train4publishing.co.uk**
Publishing	**publishing.co.uk**
Schools Register – Teaching Vacancies, etc.	**schools-register.co.uk**
Science Teaching Vacancies	**newscientist.com**
Science Technician Vacancies	**young-scientist.co.uk**
Services to Schools	**benchmarque.co.uk**
Society of Authors	**societyofauthors.org**
Supply Teacher Service	**essltd.co.uk**
Teacher Net	**teachernet.gov.uk**
Teacher Recruitment	**eteach.com**
Teacher Training Agency	**teach-tta.gov.uk**
Teaching and Projects Abroad	**teaching-abroad.co.uk**
Teaching Times	**teachingtimes.com**
University and College Lecturers' Union	**natfhe.org.uk**
Writers Guild and Society of Authors	**writers.org.uk**
Writers Guild of Great Britain	**wggb.demon.co.uk**

MUSEUMS, LIBRARIES AND HISTORY
CLCI CODES: FAE–FAH

Changes to government legislation, as well as revenue from the National Lottery, have greatly stimulated our cultural heritage. This is providing new and exciting opportunities for museums (see **museums.co.uk**), galleries and other places of cultural and historical interest. Although perhaps less funded in the public sector, fewer professions have been more influenced by new technology than librarians and information scientists. Such is the need for these skills that special recruiting agencies in knowledge management are now on the scene – see **tfpl.com**. The web is no barrier to librarians and their expertise is shared at the national consortium for public library networking at **earl.org.uk**.

The Association of Information Managers   **aslib.co.uk**

This site is a huge information resource in its own right and has everything you need to find out about the world of information management. The information resource centre includes training, on-line learning and recruitment pages.

★★   (CLCI: FAF)

Council for British Archaeology   **britarch.ac.uk**

It's great to come across a site that seems to have everything to encourage the potential archaeologist. The CBA Factsheet series (see Education) provides GCSE and A-level syllabuses, help if considering higher education and training routes as well as information about a career in archaeology. Other pages include details on grants, awards and current vacancies and much more.

★★★   (CLCI: FAH)

English Heritage   **english-heritage.org.uk**

This site warrants special mention for its excellent educational and interest value, which in any case may encourage further careers and student research. There are very good links for children and schools to explore, even taking you back in time to a virtual Stonehenge. The potential student of archaeology may find the national monument records very informative.

★   (CLCI: FAG)

History Today   **historytoday.com**

If you're interested in history, look no further than this amazing site. You can research incredible archive material on almost any given topic. The link pages reveal further gems with fascinating web sites that will take you across the globe. Just a shame there was no help on careers, but new GCSE, AS/A-Level and postgraduate information will add to the enthusiasm generated by this site.

★★   (CLCI: FAG)

Institute of Information Scientists   **iis.org.uk**

A great site if you're looking for universities that offer first degree or postgraduate courses in information science. The jobs pages will link you to newspaper vacancies and employment agencies with a specific interest in IS. The careers information is more difficult to find, but you can get a very good idea of the work by checking out the 'criteria for IS' within the Training pages.

★★   (CLCI: FAF)

Library Association	**la-hq.org.uk/careers**

I cannot rate this highly enough. The careers and qualifications pages give access to all the Library Association's current careers literature. Check out the 'day in the life' series for some brilliant profiles. There is excellent advice on training and development, and even a dedicated web site (LA jobnet) for national vacancies, and much more.

★★★ (CLCI: FAF)

Museum Training Institute	**mti.org.uk**

This site is good for NVQs/SVQs and Modern Apprenticeship information. Short on careers, but you can order free material on-line and send SAE for their free comprehensive careers brochure.

★ (CLCI: FAE)

Other Sites of Interest

Architectural Heritage Society of Scotland	**ahss.org.uk**
British Library	**bl.uk**
British Museum	**thebritishmuseum.ac.uk**
European Information Society	**http://europa.eu.int/ISPO**
Genealogical studies	**ihgs.ac.uk**
Genealogy	**genhomepage.com**
History Net	**thehistorynet.com**
Information and Library Services	**ilsnvq.org.uk**
Institute of Field Archaeologists	**archaeologists.net**
Institute of Heraldic and Genealogical Studies	**ihgs.ac.uk**
International Federation of Library Associations	**ifla.org**
Library and Information Networking	**ukoln.ac.uk**
Museum Galleries and Heritage	**24hourmuseum.org.uk**
Museum Jobs	**museumjobs.org**
Museum of Scotland	**museum.scotland.net**
Museums Association	**museumsassociation.org**
MuseumsNet	**museums.co.uk**
The National Trust	**nationaltrust.org.uk**
Northern Ireland Museums Council	**nimc.org.uk**
People's Network	**peoplesnetwork.gov.uk**
Recruitment and Consultancy to the Information Profession	**tfpl.com**
Royal Commission on the Historical Monuments	**rchme.gov.uk**
Scottish Conservation Bureau	**historic-scotland.gov.uk**
Society of Indexers	**socind.demon.co.uk**
Society of Local Archivists	**archives.org.uk**

UK Higher Education and Research
Libraries   **ex.ac.uk/library/uklibs.html**

LANGUAGES, RELIGION AND TRAINING
CLCI CODES: FAL–FAZ

Never underestimate the value of language skills in providing a passport
to a unique and exciting range of careers in the UK and, particularly,
overseas. With 2001 being declared the European Year of Languages
there is sure to be more encouragement than ever in schools and colleges
across the union. However, the site map at **cilt.org.uk** is a great place to
look at courses whatever your age! There is room for more careers-orien-
tated sites in this section, but if you are interested in teaching modern
languages then check out **international-house.org** or **canteach.gov.uk**
However, if you have a more immediate translation need and are not too
worried about it being grammatically correct, then **google.com** and
altavista.co.uk can help . If you are looking for resources including the
use of the Internet in languages, then do drop into **linguanet.org.uk**.
Anyone wanting to find out about Christian resources need look no
further than **churchnet.org.uk**. Chapter 1 covers many of the business
and management sites, some of which include training, but **videoarts.
co.uk** is a must if you want to bring humour into the equation of work-
skill training.

Catholic Online   **catholic.org**

Seems to have quite a US bias in much of the content. However, it is
still a very detailed and informative site with particularly useful pages
for student research, or exploring one's vocation, or calling, to the
Catholic faith.

★   (CLCI: FAM)

Church of England   **church-of-england.org**

If you are considering baptism or confirmation, plan to get married,
or need to make arrangements for a funeral, then you will find this site
very helpful. Should you be sensing a call to full or part-time Christian
service, then check out 'how to become more involved', which also
includes opportunities to work overseas.

★   (CLCI: FAM)

Institute of Linguists   **iol.org.uk**

This is a good site if you're looking for a linguist to help in your business. There are also useful job-hunting pages and a complete guide to examination syllabuses if you're starting out on a career using languages.

★   (CLCI: FAL)

Institute of Translation and Interpreting   **iti.org.uk**

There is sound advice at this site if you're in business and considering employing the skills of translators and interpreters. If you're thinking about careers, then check out the 'publications' page which has detailed guidance on following a career in translating and interpreting. The excellent FAQs will help further, as will Training for, a very comprehensive listing of courses at UK universities.

★★   (CLCI: FAL)

Other Sites of Interest

Association of Recognised English Language Services	**arels.org.uk**
Association of Translation Companies	**atc.org.uk**
Baptist Union	**baptist.org.uk**
Centre for Information on Language Teaching and Research	**cilt.org.uk**
CESA Language Abroad	**cesalanguages.com**
Christian Jobs Abroad	**cabroad.org.uk**
Church in Wales	**churchinwales.org.uk**
Church in Ireland	**ireland.anglican.org**
Church of Scotland	**churchofscotland.org.uk**
Conference Interpreters	**aiic.net/en/tips**
EF Global Classroom	**ef.com**
Information and Resource Contacts	**churchnet.org.uk**
Institute of IT Training	**iitt.org.uk**
International Association of Teachers of EFL	**iatefl.org**
Internet in Languages	**linguanet.org.uk**
Jewish Chronicle	**thejc.com**
Languages International	**language-international.com**
Languages Job Portal	**recruit-online.co.uk**
Methodist Church of Great Britain	**methodist.org.uk**
Quakers	**quaker.org.uk**
Salvation Army	**salvationarmy.org**
Scripture Union Resources	**scriptureunion.org.uk**
Sikh Religion	**sikhs.org**

Teacher Training Agency   **canteach.gov.uk**
Teaching of Modern Languages   **ihworld.com**
United Reformed Church   **urc.org.uk**
Video Arts   **videoarts.co.uk**
Web Enhanced Language Learning   **well.ac.uk**

The Jobs – Leisure

Actor	Musician	Dancer
Theatre Technician	Camera Operator	Director
Researcher	Film Producer	Stage Manager
Radio, Television Producer	Films and Video Editor	Arts Administrator
Leisure Centre Manager	Sports Centre Assistant	PE Teacher
Sports Development	Fitness Instructor	Groundsman
Professional Sportsman/Woman	Betting and Gaming	Sports Coach
Travel Representative	Travel Agency Assistant	Tour Manager
Travel Consultant	Hotel Manager	Receptionist
Hotel Porter	Catering Manager	Housekeeper
Restaurant Manager	Chef/Cook	Waiter/Waitress
Counter Service Assistant	Publican/Licensee	Barman/Woman
Home Economist	Cleaning Services	Refuse Collector
Beauty Therapist	Aromatherapist	Make-up Artist
Beautician	Beauty Consultant	Fashion Model
Beauty Journalism	Hairdresser	Trichologist

THEATRE, MUSIC AND DANCE
CLCI CODES: G–GAF

There is much to enjoy from the recommended site listings, but don't miss out on the gems tucked away in other less career-orientated locations. Get advice on acquiring that elusive Equity Card from **equity.org.uk** and then use their job information service or resolve that important copyright issue at **mcps.co.uk** . It may not be opera, but many dance enthusiasts will enjoy **riverdance.com** for up-to-date details on tours, family footstep pages, etc.

Association of British Theatre Technicians   **abtt.org.uk**

The Training pages provide useful link sites for both further and higher education opportunities. See Info if already involved in the profession.

★   (CLCI: GAB)

Association of Professional Recording Services   **aprs.co.uk**

You have to search hard for careers information, but an excellent site still, for anyone trying to make it in the contemporary music scene. You can link to a comprehensive list of recording studios and companies, find help if looking for a gig, and much more.

★★   (CLCI: GAD)

The BRIT School
(City College for the Technology for the Arts)   **brit.croydon.sch.uk**

You don't have to actually be at this college to benefit from the excellent help at this web site. There is an opportunity to explore a broad range of art-based careers, higher education information and job-hunting sites. Don't miss the general advice pages on music careers, though, as you will be much better informed when preparing for such a highly competitive career.

★★★   (CLCI: GAD)

Community Music   **communitymusic.org**

If you want to keep in with the community music scene in London, then look no further than this site. You will find up-to-date news of workshops, training courses and performance opportunities. Also details on lesser-known specialisms within community music, e.g. music tutor training and music and technology courses. For wider national and particularly disabled support, check out **soundsense.org**

★★   (CLCI: GAD)

Incorporated Society of Musicians   **ism.org**

Be encouraged by the wealth of material that pours out of this site. The Information Sheets take you to an excellent series of Careers in Music pages that cover everything from performing, composing and music therapy, to educational routes and training, and much more besides! The ISM's excellent Careers in Music publication is available free on-line. There is little on the Internet about work experience, but you will find here a list of possible opportunities with the ISM's own corporate members. You can also visit the edited highlights of the current *Musical Journal* to see whether it's worth purchasing.

★★★   (CLCI: GAD)

Metier Arts and Entertainment Industry   **metier.org.uk**

See Careers and Guidance for access to useful details and contact information for careers in music and the theatre. Also Learning and Skills pages for GNVQ support material. Metier is the national training organisation (NTO) which represents over 500,000 people in the performing, visual, literary, teaching, administration and technical arts.

★★   (CLCI: G)

Music Education Directory   **bpi-med.co.uk**

The Industry Maps and Courses pages is a great place to start if you are researching or wishing to work in the music industry. See the Industry Organisation pages for useful links to related sectors.

★★   (CLCI: GAD)

National Council for Drama   **ncdt.co.uk**

An essential site for the genuine aspiring drama student with excellent education, training and a unique graduate database. The drama links will also encourage your research and job-hunting prospects.

★★   (CLCI: GAB)

Royal Opera House   **royalopera.org**

This site is particularly rated for its educational value and excellent insights into the world of ballet, opera and orchestra at The Royal Opera House. There is much for the young enthusiast or teacher to adapt for the classroom, as well the seasoned lover of such arts who wants to be kept informed of all the events and news.

★   (CLCI: GAF)

The Stage Weekly Journal   **thestage.co.uk**

The Auditions, Recruitment and Jobs pages will keep you well informed on a wide range of creative jobs; from work in the theatre itself, to holiday club compères and writing for TV and radio.

★   (CLCI: GAB)

UK Theatre Web	uktw.co.uk

Some useful information on jobs and training particularly for technicians and stage managers, who can also submit their CV by e-mail for potential vacancies. However, this is a great site if wishing to explore the whole area of performing arts. There are links to the lesser known skills of clowning, but also to the UK Actors Directory and the major film distributors web sites.

★★ (CLCI: GAB)

Other Sites of Interest

The Actors Directory	the-actors-directory.com
All About Jazz (USA)	allaboutjazz.com
Art Guide	artguide.org
Arts and Entertainment Industry	netgain.org.uk
British Academy of Composers and Songwriters	britishacademy.com
British Actors Equity Association	equity.org.uk
British Film Institute	bfi.org.uk
British Society of Music Therapy	bsmt.org
Business Training for the Music Industry	mbr.mcmail.com
Conference of Drama Schools	drama.ac.uk
English National Ballet	ballet.org.uk
Film and Screen Writers Network	shootingpeople.com
Imperial Society of Teachers of Dancing	istd.org
Institute of Popular Music	liv.ac.uk
International Managers Forum	imf-uk.org/
Laban Centre Dance	laban.co.uk
Live Music Industry	musicbank.org
Liverpool Institute for Performing Arts	lipa.ac.uk
London Music School	tlms.co.uk
Mechanical Copyright Protection Society	mcps.co.uk
Mime and Physical Theatre	mime.org.uk
Music Industry Directory	music-media.co.uk
National Association of Youth Theatres	nayt.org.uk
National Council for Drama Training	ncdt.co.uk
National Resource Centre for Dance	surrey.ac.uk/NRCD
National Youth Theatre	nyt.org.uk
Performing Rights Society	prs.co.uk
Register of Consultants and Trainers in the Arts	arts-consultants.org.uk
Riverdance	riverdance.com
Royal Academy of Dance	rad.org.uk
Royal College of Music	rcm.ac.uk

Royal Northern College of Music	**rncm.ac.uk**
Royal Scottish Academy of Music and Drama	**rsamd.ac.uk**
Royal Shakespeare Company	**rsc.org.uk**
Scottish Arts Council	**sac.org.uk**
Showcase International Music Book	**showcase-music.com**
Spotlight Casting Directory	**spotlightcd.com**
Stage Register	**stageregister.com**
Theatre Personnel Nationwide	**tpn.org.uk**
University Drama Departments (SCUDD)	**http://art.ntu.ac.uk/scudd**
What's On Stage	**whatsonstage.com**

SPORT, OUTDOOR PURSUITS AND RECREATIONAL MANAGEMENT
CLCI CODES: GAG-GAK

The nation's love of sport enters an exciting era with the Internet's ability to provide a wide range of instant up-to-date sports information. The new medium is also providing easier access to details on education and training for what is increasingly becoming one of the fastest growing employment sectors. Perhaps you're having difficulty financing your coaching or training needs. Sports Aid at **sportsaid.org.uk** is a great place to start. If you are not destined for professional sport, but would love to be part of one of Britain's fastest growing industries, why not check out a career in sport and recreational management at **isrm.co.uk**.

British Horseracing Board   **bhb.co.uk**

You can access some very good information from the Careers Training pages. Short on job information, but a good site for anyone interested in finding out what the world of racing is all about.

★★   (CLCI: GAG)

English Sports Council   **sportengland.org**

If you like sport then you're in for a treat here. There are link pages which take you to nearly all the main sporting web sites, but I recommend you first visit Site Topics A–Z, as it will be easy to miss the hidden gems including the informative careers in sport pages!

★★★   (CLCI: GAG)

Institute of Leisure and Amenity Management	**ilam.co.uk**

There are some excellent career pages tucked within Education and Training, including a 28-page careers in leisure guide. Also at 'jobs' you can get some idea of salaries in the industry. However, you need to subscribe to the appointment service or journal, to get more information on specific vacancies.

★★ (CLCI: GAJ)

Sports Coach UK	**sportscoachuk.org**

This newly named organisation, formerly the National Coaching Foundation, provides a great springboard to a career in coaching. The links are great, but the real gem is in the factsheet series you can download from the student pages.

★★ (CLCI: GAG)

UK Sport	**uksport.gov.uk**

Whether you are a sports enthusiast, or keen to pursue an amateur or professional career in sport, you will want to keep coming back to this excellent site. It's packed with topical news stories, a brilliant Sport A–Z, job-hunting pages and much more!

★★ (CLCI: GAG)

Other Sites of Interest

Athletics Net	**athleticsnet.com**
BBC Sport	**http://news.bbc.co.uk/sport/**
British Association of Sport and Exercise Sciences	**bases.org.uk**
British Athletics	**british-athletics.co.uk**
British Council for Chinese Martial Arts	**bccma.org.uk**
British Olympic Association	**olympics.org.uk**
British Paralympic Association	**paralympics.org.uk**
Department for Culture, Media and Sport	**culture.gov.uk**
First Eleven Sports Agency	**firsteleven.co.uk**
Gatorade Sports Science Institute (USA)	**gssiweb.com**
Institute of Sport and Recreation Management	**isrm.co.uk**
Ladbrokes	**ladbrokes.co.uk**
Mad On Sport	**madonsport.com**
National Playing Fields Association	**nfpa.co.uk**
National Sports Medicine Institute	**nsmi.org.uk**
Popular Flying Association	**pfa.org.uk**

Professional Golfers' Association	**pga.org.uk**
Real Runner	**realrunner.com**
Royal Yachting Association	**rya.org.uk**
Scottish Athletic Association	**saf.org.uk**
Sport and Recreation	**sprito.org.uk**
Sport Scotland	**sportscotland.org.uk**
Sports Aid	**sportsaid.org.uk**
Sports Coach UK	**sportscoachuk.org**
Sports Council for Northern Ireland	**sportni.org**
Sports Council for Wales	**sports-council-wales.co.uk**
Sub Aqua Association	**saa.org.uk**
Swimming Training Association	**sta.co.uk**
UK Sailing Academy	**uk-sail.org.uk**
UK Sport	**uksport.gov.uk**
Watersport Training	**flyfishingonline.com**
Women's Sports Foundation	**wsf.org.uk**
Yachting	**yacht.co.uk**

RADIO, TV, FILMS, VIDEO AND ENTERTAINMENT
CLCI CODES: GAL-GAV

There is much useful research you can undertake here in relation to careers in television by checking out the BBC, or any one of the independent regional companies from **itv.co.uk**. There is also the latest on the film industry and its associated glitz and glamour at **popcorn.co.uk**. If you are a budding cartoonist, you may well be inspired at **animaart.com** which is an on-line Animation Art Gallery. The leisure industry is continuing to grow at a pace as we embark on the new century and if you are thinking about a holiday job or entering this exciting career, then the Disney Corporation at **disney.com** will be worth a visit, in addition to other theme parks listed in this section. The first steps towards a career in clowning or puppetry may start with **clowning.u-net.com** and **puppco.demon.co.uk**. For circus life try **thecircusspace.co.uk**

BBC   **bbc.co.uk/jobs**

This is a highly rated site for anyone seeking a career in broadcasting including journalism, programme making, business support and management, and much more. Job seekers and work experience applicants can check out the positions vacant pages, if aged 15–18.
★★★   (CLCI: GAL)

British Kinematograph Sound and Television Society   **bksts.com**

From the home page drop down to the excellent and wide ranging Careers in Film and Television, you would be hard pressed getting such valuable insights elsewhere and if still keen check out the helpful tips on what to look out for in a media course.

★★   (CLCI: GAL)

Broadcast Journalism Training Council   **bjtc.org.uk**

All the encouragement you need on training to be a broadcast journalist is on this site. The FAQs are certainly worth a visit and there is plenty of course information and links to college sites for even more detail. There is even advice for course leaders and colleges considering starting courses.

★★   (CLCI: GAL)

Broadcast, Film, Video & Interactive Media   **skillset.org**

I cannot rate this site highly enough and that is without referring to the new and exciting **skillsformedia.com** pages which were under development at the time of writing. Don't miss the excellent links to other web sites. I stopped counting at 50!

★★★   (CLCL: GAL)

Lighting Design   **ald.org.uk**

Limited careers information on this specialist field, but the Corporates pages may well kickstart your career with links to potential employers in the lighting industry. The Forum pages also look useful, but you need to be a member to get full benefit from this site.

★   (CLCI: GAT)

Online Regional Arts Pages   **arts.org.uk**

You must get immersed in this excellent site. If you are at an early stage in your career ideas, thinking seriously about courses to encourage your creative interest, or using your skills to find work, you will get great advice here. The site is also designed (text-only browser) to help the visually impaired locate the same information. You can search on all the main art disciplines, from dance to craft, as well as further web and e-mail links. Searching by regions is painless, and the training pages will help you research the right courses including part-time, further and higher education. There is excellent advice on funding, and the business pages will be a great encouragement to those preferring to be, or having to be, self-employed.

★★★ (CLCI: GAL)

Produxion Line **produxion.com**

Once registered into Produxion Line you can access the UK's most comprehensive on-line database for UK television production, including over 13,000 contacts for companies and freelancers.

★★ (CLCI: GAL)

The Society of British Theatre Design **theatredesign.org.uk**

See Training pages for details on a wide range of theatre-related courses, including lighting, costume, front of house operations, set design, sound and stage management. Links pages also look useful.

★ (CLCI: GAT)

Thorpe Park **thorpepark.co.uk**

A fun site to visit in any case. However, very handy if you are currently studying for a qualification in leisure and tourism. Check out the recruitment pages for details on seasonal, permanent and work placement opportunities at Thorpe Park and Chessington World of Adventures.

★ (CLCI: GAN)

Other Sites of Interest

Alton Towers	**alton-towers.co.uk**
Animation Art Gallery	**animaart.com**
Animation UK Magazine	**animationuk.com**
British Film Institute	**bfi.org.uk**
Broadcasting Entertainment Cinematograph & Theatre Union	**bectu.org.uk**
Carlton TV	**carlton.co.uk**
Channel 4	**channel4.com**
Digital Radio	**ukdigitalradio.com**

Disney	**disney.com**
Hospital Broadcasting Association	**hbauk.com**
ITV	**itv.co.uk**
Living Spirit	**livingspirit.com**
Movies	**popcorn.co.uk**
Producers Alliance for Cinema and Television	**pact.co.uk**
Radio Authority	**radioauthority.org.uk**
Science Broadcasting	**vega.org.uk**
Video Arts	**videoarts.co.uk**

TRAVEL AND TOURISM, HOTEL AND CATERING
CLCI CODES: GAX-IC

The travel, tourism and associated hotel and catering industries are among the UK's biggest employers, currently about 10% of the workforce and estimated to rise by over 400,000 by 2006 (source: Henley Centre for Forecasting). It is therefore no surprise that this section has so many good quality sites. In addition, there are still gems hidden in others. For example, if you like the idea of being a registered tour guide, then check out **blue-badge.org.uk**. There is always the possibility of jet-setting with **atme.org** which will be of particular interest to travel marketing executives and students wishing to keep up to date with the latest tips and trends in the industry. If you are a student or journalist researching hospitality careers then **bha-online.org.uk** will be a very useful place to start, but also take a glance at **hcareers.co.uk** and **hospitalitymoves.com**. Should there be more appeal towards the international hotel and restaurant scene, what better site to be informed from than **ih-ra.com**. Certainly disabled people seeking accommodation will be encouraged by the list of over 2,000 hotels hosted at **allgohere.com**.

Brewers and Licensed Retailers Association **blra.co.uk**

Superb site with everything you need to know about careers in licensed retailing, brewing, running a pub and much more besides! Qualifications are also well covered and there are further contacts and web sites to help your research.

★★★ (CLCI: I)

British Airways **britishairwaysjobs.com**

Very impressive careers and recruitment information await you at British Airways. There are details on a wide range of employment possibilities whether you are a graduate, potential pilot or engineer, interested in cabin crew, or supporting worldwide cargo operations. Don't miss the FAQs and there are some very helpful tips on preparing your CV. The world's largest airline is living up to its name.

★★★ (CLCI: GAX)

Centre for Contemporary Circus and Physical Performance   **circomedia.com**

This is more like a college prospectus, but still a great introduction to many of the lesser-known, yet highly skilled circus crafts. Short on careers information, although the ex-student pages make interesting reading as well as 'where do our graduates work' which are tucked within courses information.

★ (CLCI: GAZ)

Food Jobs   **foodjobs.co.uk**

Essentially a job-hunting site for a range of careers, which at the time of writing were mainly at middle and senior management level.

★ (CLCI: I)

Hospitality Training Foundation   **htf.org.uk**

Very good information on training and qualification routes into the industry including NVQ/SVQs and Modern Apprenticeships. The site also includes an excellent course finder map to locate opportunities to train at college and university.

★★ (CLCI: IB)

Hotel and Catering International Management Association   **hcima.org.uk**

It seems you have to sign up as a member in order to get the full benefits from this site. However, there are still excellent features within the news and professional development pages, with opportunities for flexi-study and distance learning. HCIMA diploma and certificate courses are also listed.

★ (CLCI: IB)

Leisure Careers   **barzone.co.uk**

The Career, and Job and Work Zones guide you into a wealth of information and potential opportunities. Career Zone has an excellent explanation of the qualification structure of the industry, valuable personal experiences listed within case studies, as well as helpful resources for careers teachers. Job Zone's gems include registering your CV on-line and finding employment, while the Work Zone's unique contribution covers those sometimes elusive openings to gain valuable work experience.

★★★   (CLCI: IB)

Springboard UK   **careercompass.co.uk**

This site has excellent links to job-hunting opportunities in the hospitality, leisure and tourism industries. It is highly rated for its course finder, links and skills match programme which tests out your potential interest in this diverse and exciting employment sector. 'Top Tips' advice section such as writing CVs (three examples given) and interview advice. Inspiring but very brief information on careers in the hospitality, leisure and tourism industries.

★★★   (CLCI: IB/IC)

The Travel Training Company   **tttc.co.uk**

This site offers a good introduction to a broad range of careers in the travel industry. See the FAQs on interests such as, 'how to become a resort representative', or 'setting up your own travel agency'. There are also useful pages at Training Matters with details on courses and qualifications to get you started.

★★   (CLCI: GAX)

Other Sites of Interest

Association of British Travel Agents	**abtanet.com**
Association of Travel Marketing Executives	**atme.org**
British Hospitality Association	**bha-online.org.uk**
British Institute of Innkeeping	**bii.org**
British Tourist Authority	**visitbritain.com**
Caterer	**caterer.com**
Catering Net	**cateringnet.co.uk**
Cordonbleu	**cordonbleu.net**
English Tourist Board	**travelengland.org.uk**
Food and Wine (private school)	**leiths.com**

Guild of British Travel Agents	**gbta-guild.com**
Guild of Registered Tourist Guides	**blue-badge.org.uk/guild**
Hospitality and Tourism Trends	**whatt.net**
Info Travel	**infotravel.co.uk**
International Hotel and Restaurant Association	**ih-ra.com**
Ireland Travel	**ireland.travel.ie**
Thomas Cook	**thomascook.co.uk**
Virgin Airways	**virgin.com**
Wine and Spirit Education Trust	**wset.co.uk**
World Travel and Tourism Council	**wttc.org**

CLEANING SERVICES AND BEAUTY CULTURE
CLCI CODES: ID–IZ

Few of us probably ever think of the huge army, estimated at nearly one million dedicated personnel, involved in cleaning, caretaking and attendant work in schools, hospitals and businesses across the nation; often unglamorous work with very unsociable hours. In complete contrast, the beauty industry attracts much media interest as well as a growing number of Internet sites. This section should be explored along with fashion (see EJ) as there is much overlap between beauty and fashion-related careers.

Guild of Professional Beauty Therapists	**beauty-guild.co.uk**

See the Guild's own Beauty Recruitment Agency for excellent listing of current vacancies across a broad range of careers within beauty therapy. Also check within the Training Directory for an impressive list of colleges offering beauty and holistic therapy courses nationally. Little careers information, but this site does link to others, for example **beautyserve.com**, with its salon finder facility, which you could also use to seek work experience or potential employment opportunities.

★ (CLCI: IK)

Hairdressing and Beauty Industry Authority	**habia.org.uk**

The careers and training information for hairdressing is particularly good at this site. Seek out the 'drop down' menus within FAQs. The Post Graduate Information may be a little misleading as this is not normally degree entry, but nevertheless you will find some excellent advice on the opportunities and qualities needed to work at the more competitive edge of the industry, e.g. a training consultant, in films or on cruise liners. Not the easiest site to navigate, so if you do get stuck, as I did looking for the popular 'Chair Renting' option for experienced Hairdressers, use the search page.

★★ (CLCI: IK / IL)

Broadcast, Film, Video & Interactive Media   skillset.org

I cannot rate this site highly enough and that is without referring to the new and exciting **skillsformedia.com** pages which were under development at the time of writing. Don't miss the links to other web sites, which are excellent – I stopped counting at 50.

★★★ (CLCI: GAL)

Virgin   virgin.co.uk

As one might expect, this is a highly imaginative and presentable site packed with travel and retail information and offers. However, the jobs pages link to current recruitment opportunities within the whole organisation and the impressive list of Virgin companies will certainly give you a taste for working with one of Britain's most admired entrepreneurs, Sir Richard Branson.

★ (CLCI: IK)

Other Sites of Interest

British Pest Control Association	**bpca.org.uk**
Cleaning Association	**cleaningassociation.org**
Fashion Net	**fashion.net**
Fashion Modelling	**models.co.uk**
Hair World	**hairworld.com**
Salon Net	**salon.net**

3
Medical, Health
and Social Care

Few careers can be more rewarding or satisfying than delivering or saving a life, saving a marriage, caring for the disadvantaged, or helping someone suffering from great anxiety. Such careers at life's sharp end are not for the faint-hearted, as one minute you could be carrying out a routine task and the next thrown into a harrowing emergency in which you have to react with great skill. For every medical specialist and counsellor working directly with the public, there are an equal number of dedicated health care professionals, scientists and counsellors also contributing significantly to the nation's physical and emotional well-being. Jobs and work practices in this sector are constantly changing, with increased demands on efficiency and accurate record-keeping, as well as greater fears of litigation. However, it is also a very exciting area to work in, with discoveries in medical science and technology encouraging further opportunities for specialisation and even new careers.

Skills and Interests
Most jobs are team based, often working alongside or relying on other specialists, but many of the personal qualities and skills listed below will be common. What is interesting is the number of attributes that are natural, almost instinctive, and therefore perhaps worth closer careers investigation.

- Sensitive, caring, friendly and reliable.
- Patient and relate well to different people.
- Good listener, compassionate, trustworthy and discreet.
- Practical and physically fit.
- Mature with initiative and commitment.
- Team player, but capable of working independently.
- Interest in science.
- Well organised, communication skills and a good sense of humour.
- Business skills and technically adept.

Organisations and Work Environment

NHS hospitals, private clinics, health centres and GP surgeries, hospices, armed forces, community centres, educational establishments, industry, relief agencies, charities and voluntary bodies, dental community services, clinics and hospitals, research centres and laboratories, pharmacies, retail outlets, sports centres, clubs and gyms, treatment units, ambulance service, private homes, nurseries and day centres, social services youth clubs, residential homes, courts, HM prisons, careers companies and employment agencies.

The Jobs

Hospital Doctor	General Practitioner	Medical Officer
Nurse	Midwife	Health Visitor
District Nurse	Sick Children's Nurse	Health Care Assistant
Occupational Health Nurse	Health Education Officer	Dentist
Dental Nurse	Dental Technician	Dental Therapist
Dental Hygienist	Dental Receptionist	Medical Secretary
Pharmacist	Pharmacy Technician	Optometrist
Optician	Orthoptist	Physiotherapist
Radiographer	Occupational Therapist	Chiropodist
Medical Research	Ambulance Work	Acupuncturist
Chiropractor	Homoeopath	Reflexologist
Herbalist	Osteopath	Prosthetics
Careers Adviser	Counsellor	Social Worker
Youth Worker	Psychologist	Speech and Language
Dietician	Music Therapist	Therapist

MEDICINE, SURGERY, NURSING, DENTISTRY, PHARMACY AND OPHTHALMICS
CLCI CODES: J–JAL

As well as the star-rated career gems below, you may wish to pursue your interest by visiting professional magazines such as *Health Service Journal* at **hsi.co.uk** and *Nursing Times* at **nursingtimes.net**. You may need to register your details to get full access to job information. At the time of writing **nhscareers.nhs.uk** was under development. If you are an experienced nurse but ready for a fresh start, check out the highly impressive **british-nursing.com** for a portfolio of major nursing sites and job vacancies. Also of note is the UKCC but suggest visiting the site map and FAQs for the real gems. For education and interest you can always go international with the US government's Food and Drug Administration at **fda.gov**.

British Dental Association   **bda-dentistry.org.uk**

There is a healthy range of material within the Public pages and careers in dentistry in particular. Also an extremely useful guide for overseas dentists wishing to practise in the UK. You will be amazed at the link pages (see BDA Directory), which include research sites, the lucrative but little-known Dental Trade businesses, as well as overseas associations. I recommend also complementing your research by checking the British Dental Practice Managers Association web site which has further careers information and good educational resource pages.

★★★   (CLCI: JAF)

British Medical Association   **bma.org.uk**

This is an excellent site packed with useful information, although some topics will require password entry. However, if you're an aspiring medical student, then do drop into the careers and education pages and the specific section on becoming a doctor. It includes advice for mature and graduate applicants, as well as students with disabilities.

★★★   (CLCI: JAB)

British Medical Journal   **bmj.com**

The Classified Ads pages are your link to medical vacancies covering anything from family planning and public health, to community health and appointments in the armed forces. At the time of writing there were over 1,500 vacancies advertised. Aspiring medical students may benefit from visiting the Careers Focus series of articles on past journals. At the very least you will be in a better position to ask more informed questions, should you be fortunate enough get as far as the interview stage for this highly sought-after profession.

★★   (CLCI: JAB)

The College of Optometrists   **college-optometrists.org**

The Public and Training pages will support your careers research and there is plenty of good information to find, including a number of careers associated with eye care. The link pages lead to further web sites, as well as other educational institutions for course information.

★★   (CLCI: JAL)

English National Board for Nursing, Midwifery and Health   enb.org.uk

Do not be put off by the rather uninspiring presentation of this site, it is packed with useful information and link pages to related information. The Pre-Registration pages within ENB Programmes are good if you're considering a career in nursing and midwifery. The Practice pages cover other specialisms and Research and Development may appeal more to the established career professional.
★★ (CLCI: JAD)

National Board for Nursing, Midwifery and Health Visiting in Scotland   nbs.org.uk

This Scottish site includes a brief introduction to nursing. There is much more emphasis on the application process and support from the National Board.
★ (CLCI: JAD)

NHS Careers   nhscareers.nhs.uk

Brilliant! It is great to come across such an informative and helpful site that is dedicated to careers in nursing, the allied health professions and healthcare services. There is also encouraging advice for those already trained, but who perhaps instinctively sense a need to return to their vocation.
★★★ (CLCI: JAD)

Nursing and Midwifery Admissions Service   nmas.ac.uk

If you are looking to pursue nursing or midwifery studies then you can enjoy checking out the main directory of courses on this site. There are also links directly to university and college web sites for more detail on courses. Application procedures can be explored further and information packs sent to your home.
★ (CLCI: JAD)

Pharmaceutical Information   pharmweb.net

This looks to be a particularly good site for those already established in the profession. The drop down menu from the home page with access to the site index is a good place to start as you then can search topics of interest from the highly impressive A–Z listing. A little short on careers information and so you may have to access a few university sites to get more detail. However, there is much to interest the aspiring pharmacist and an excellent international site if looking for work outside the UK. Look out for new version 2 which was under development at the time of writing.

★   (CLCI: JAG)

Pharmacy	**askyourpharmacist.co.uk**

Includes useful but limited careers information, as well as details on the personal skills required to work in pharmacy. This is, however, a very good site for general enquiries that members of the public may have, and so may help you to be better informed if you are going for an interview.

★   (CLCI: JAG)

Royal College of Midwives Journal	**midwives.co.uk**

Although you can search for jobs in this site the emphasis is much more on supporting the professionally qualified midwife than attracting potential applicants.

★   (CLCI: JAD)

Royal College of Ophthalmologists	**rcophth.ac.uk**

The site map will link you to the education and training pages for a very detailed introduction to a career in ophthalmology.

★★   (CLCI: JAL)

Royal College of Surgeons	**rcseng.ac.uk**

Visit the site menu and training to locate the Careers Advice and Career Path pages for an excellent introduction to this specialist area of medicine.

★★   (CLCI: JAB)

UK Health Centre	**healthcentre.org.uk**

This is a great example of professional information getting into the public arena. This site is packed with brilliant easy-to-locate web links to just about every source of medical information. You need to go into Staff Room for a very impressive range of further vacancy pages.

★★   (CLCI: J)

Welsh National Board for Nursing, Midwifery and Health Visiting **wnb.org.uk**

This bilingual site includes an attractive series of careers information sheets. They cover initial entry to the profession, continuing professional development and advice for returners or overseas applicants to nursing.

★★ (CLCI: JAD)

Other Sites of Interest

Active for Live	**active.org.uk**
The Association of Operating Department Practitioners	**aodp.org**
Association of Optometrists	**assocoptom.co.uk**
British Dental Practice Managers Association	**bdpma.org**
British Dental Trade Association	**bdta.org.uk**
Dental Laboratories Association	**dla.org.uk**
Department of Health	**doh.gov.uk**
Food and Drug Administration (USA)	**fda.gov**
General Dental Council	**gdc-uk.org**
General Optical Council	**optical.org**
HealthProfessional	**healthprofessionals.com**
Health Service Journal	**hsj.co.uk**
Institute of Psychiatry	**iop.kcl.ac.uk**
Internet Mental Health	**mentalhealth.com**
Mental Help Nt (US)	**mentalhelp.net**
National Board for Nursing, Midwifery and Health Visiting for Northern Ireland	**n-i.nhs.uk/NBNI/index.html**
National Eye Research Centre	**nerc.co.uk**
National Pharmaceutial Association	**npa.co.uk**
National Sports Medicine Institute	**nsmi.org.uk**
NHS Careers	**nhscareers.nhs.uk**
NHS Direct	**nhsdirect.nhs.uk**
NHS Northern Ireland	**n-i.nhs.uk**
Nurse Bank – London	**nursebank.co.uk**
Nurse Serve	**nurserve.co.uk**
Nursing Net	**nursingnet.uk**
Nursing Standard	**nursing-standard.co.uk**
Nursing Websites and Vacancies	**british-nursing.com**
Organising Medical Networked Information	**omni.ac.uk**
The Queen's Nursing Institute Scotland	**qnis.co.uk**
Royal College of Nursing	**rcn.org.uk**
Royal College of Psychiatrists	**rcpsych.ac.uk**

Royal Society of Medicine   **roysocmed.ac.uk**
UK Central Council for Nursing, Midwifery and
  Health Visiting   **ukcc.org.uk**

PHYSIOTHERAPY, RADIOGRAPHY, SPEECH THERAPY AND CHIROPODY
CLCI CODES: JAN–JAT

Some of the smaller and more specialised health disciplines have yet to develop their web sites to their full career potential. However, there are still gems found in this part of the maze to support your research such as **cpsm.org.uk** and information about complementary medicine, which spans a number of sections in this book. You can find a local chiropodist at **feetforlife.org/careers**, as well as help with foot health information and specialist advice for children, diabetics and sports enthusiasts.

Chartered Society of Physiotherapy   **csp.org.uk**

Last year more applicants applied for degree courses than any other subject in terms of applicants per place. So, good careers and course research complemented by related work experience should help towards this highly competitive profession. The site holds useful educational information, but currently you have to send for the careers guide. The site includes an on-line recruitment section, fact sheets on working in Australia and New Zealand, as well as help for overseas applicants wishing to practise in the UK.

★   (CLCI: JAN)

College of Occupational Therapists   **cot.co.uk**

At the time of writing this site was undergoing a major development, so it will be interesting to see how it can better its three-star rating from the previous edition!

★★★   (CLCI: JAR)

Royal College of Speech and Language Therapy   **rcslt.org**

This is a helpful site whether you are a seasoned expert looking to return to the profession, or a student searching potential undergraduate or postgraduate courses. Sadly though, a little thin on careers information.

★   (CLCI: JAS)

Other Sites of Interest

British Institute of Radiology	**bir.org.uk**
Chartered Society of Physiotherapy	**csp.org.uk**
Council for Professions Supplementary to Medicine	**cpsm.org.uk**
Royal College of Speech and Language Therapists	**rcslt.org**
Society of Radiographers	**sor.org**
Society of Chiropodists and Podiatrists	**feetforlife.org**

DIETETICS, AMBULANCE WORK AND COMPLEMENTARY MEDICINE
CLCI CODES: JAV–JOZ

There is no shortage of sites, but you may have to research further for careers information at your local careers office or write/send an e-mail to the organisations of interest. County ambulance sites are worth checking at **ambulance.co.uk**. If you or your children have suffered from disorders related to hearing and balance, you may be interested in the work of audiological physicians at **baap.org.uk**. For care and advice on rehabilitation and special products to relieve discomfort, visit the little known but vital services provided by Prosthetists and Orthotists at **bapo.com**.

Association of Professional Music Therapists   **www.apmt.org.uk**

This site is just packed with helpful information, particularly if you're exploring the potential use of music therapy. This includes brief but useful careers information and further associated web sites such as the British Society for Music Therapy at **bsmt.org**.

★   (CLCI: JOD)

British College of Naturopathy & Osteopathy   **bcno.org.uk**

Little careers information, but still a useful site with helpful background detail to this specialist area in complementary medicine. You can research course information at a number of institutions that run BSc or MSc study options.

★   (CLCI: JOD)

Dietetics   **bda.uk.com**

The education and training pages hold most of the careers and course information. There are also helpful details on postgraduate, clinical placements and continual professional development for those newly arrived as well as those established in their careers. An impressive national vacancy list for dietitians can be located in List all jobs.

★★ (CLCI: JAV)

Institute of Physics & Engineering in Medicine **ipem.org.uk**

You will find little careers information at this site, but it is the Jobs in Medical Physics and Engineering pages which demonstrate more conclusively the types of medical related work undertaken.

★ (CLCI: JOB)

Other Sites of Interest

Anglo European College of Chiropractic	**aecc.ac.uk**
Association of Reflexologists	**reflexology.org**
British Acupuncture Council	**demon.co.uk/acupuncture/bacc.html**
British Association of Audiological Physicians	**baap.org.uk**
British Association of Music Therapy	
	around.ntl.sympatico.ca/~a815music.htm
British Association of Prosthetics and Orthotics	**bapo.com**
British Association of Public Safety Communications	
Officers	**babco.org.uk**
British Chiropractic Association	**chiropractic-uk.co.uk**
British Osteopathic Association	**osteopathy.org.uk**
British Society of Audiology	**b-s-a.demon.co.uk**
British Society for Music Therapy	**bsmt.org**
County Ambulance Services	**ambulance.co.uk**
International Committee of the Red Cross	**icrc.org**
National Association of Air Ambulance Services	**naaas.co.uk**
National Centre for Training and Education	
in Prosthetics and Orthotics	**strath.ac.uk/Departments/NatCentre**
National Play Information Centre	**npfa.co.uk**
Prosthetics and Orthotics	**salford.ac.uk/prosthetic**
Science Technician Vacancies	**young-scientist.co.uk**
World Health Organisation	**who.int**

SOCIAL CARE, CAREERS ADVICE, YOUTH AND COMMUNITY
CLCI CODES: K–KEG

This sector is going through considerable change as child care, adoption and fostering services all become more regulated, in order to achieve higher standards of care for the young and vulnerable in our society. This is potentially good for those wishing to work in this diverse field as the quality of training also falls under the microscope. There are some very good career sites here, such as **intercarenet.co.uk** if you want to work in (or are looking for care of relatives in) a nursing home or residential care home. By contrast, government policy on the new careers connections service for young people can be explored at **connexions.gov.uk**. However, it will be good to bookmark the complementary **connexionscard.com** as this site is currently updating a number of commercial publications for free access on the Internet. Should you want to go a stage further in the theories of careers guidance, then **derby.ac.uk/cegs** is certainly worth a browse. Not sure of the life span of this site promoting this International Year of Volunteers, but looks worth a visit at **iyv2001.org**.

Careers Service National Association   careers-uk.com

The links pages will take you to a wealth of useful education, training, employment, guidance and careers information sources. Why not also check out the careers advice pages to locate your own careers organisations and the services they offer?

★   (CLCI: KED)

Child Care & Education   cache.org.uk

The Council for Wards in Children's Care and Education (CACHE) is concerned with the development of courses and qualifications for people who work, or plan to work, with children and young people. The careers information is brief but useful, outlining a number of work situations that one can specialise in. FAQ and Resource pages were under development at the time of writing.

★★   (CLCI: KEB)

The Princess Royal Trust for Carers   carers.org

This home page provides a useful definition of the role of a carer, as well as topical issues in the press. However, this site is noted for its excellent links to related health and care organisations, which can be found within Other Sites.

★   (CLCI: KEB)

Social Work	**ccetsw.org.uk**

The FAQs are certainly worth a visit, particularly if you want to find out about social work qualifications. There are some very useful careers pages which can be found in the 'download area'.

★★ (CLCI: KEB)

University of Northumbria at Newcastle	**unn.ac.uk/academic/hswe/careers**

This site is great fun if you're thinking about becoming a careers adviser. There is plenty of helpful information on training and funding, the job itself, as well as prospects for employment. However, I do recommend you visit L plate pages, as this will give you a great insight into the resources that students can call upon to help their studies and work practice.

★★ (CLCI: KED)

Other Sites of Interest

Au Pair America	**aifs.com/aupair_intl/**
British Association of Social Workers	**basw.co.uk**
Centre for Guidance Studies	**derby.ac.uk/cegs**
Child Care Education	**cache.org.uk**
Children's Society	**the-childrens-society.org.uk**
College of Guidance Studies	**cogs.ac.uk**
Community Based Learning and Development	**paulo.org.uk**
DHSS and Public Safety – Northern Ireland	**dhsspsni.gov.uk**
Department of Social Security	**dss.gov.uk**
European Social Fund	**esfnews.org.uk**
Institute of Careers Guidance	**icg-uk.org**
International Childcare Trust	**ict-uk.org**
International Au Pair Work	**aupairs.co.uk**
Kindercare Independent Fostering Agency	**kindercare.co.uk**
The National Association of Careers and Guidance Teachers	**nacgt.org.uk**
National Children's Bureau	**ncb.org.uk**
National Institution of Social Work	**nisw.org.uk**
National Play Information Centre	**npfa.co.uk**
National Society for the Prevention of Cruelty to Children	**nspcc.org.uk**
National Training Organisation for Early Years	**early-years-nto.org.uk**
NCH Action for Children	**nchafc.org.uk**
Norland Nannies	**norland.co.uk**

Nursing Homes and Residential Care Homes
  in the UK   **intercarenet.co.uk**
Probation Practice   **mailbase.ac.uk/lists/probation-practice**
Professional Association of Nursery Nurses   **pat.org.uk**
Search 4 Social Workers   **search4socialworkers.com**
Social Science Gateway   **sosig.ac.uk**
Social Services   **topss.org.uk**
Social Work Recruitment Specialists   **careplan.co.uk**
Sociology Central (A-level sociology students and
  teachers)   **sociology.org.uk**
Tavistock Institute   **tavinstitute.org**
YouthOrg UK   **youth.org.uk**

COUNSELLING, PSYCHOLOGY, CHARITIES AND VOLUNTARY ORGANISATIONS
CLCI CODES: KEK–KEZ

More detail follows on some of the prime sites for careers information in this sector. However, perhaps you are at a stage in your life where you're looking to use your considerable personal life skills to help and encourage others either in paid employment or in some kind of voluntary capacity. If you want to gain formal counselling qualifications, look no further than **bac.co.uk**. Here you will find a list of the basic principles of counselling which may help in your planning, as well as advice on courses and training. You are spoilt for choice on the voluntary side, but most scouting organisations at **scoutbase.org.uk** would benefit greatly from more support. Another national institution is Barnardo's, which is the UK's largest children's charity. You can explore a number of interesting pages at **barnardos.org.uk** including news of current campaigns and the opportunity again to get involved.

British Psychological Society   **bps.org.uk**

Check out the careers and development pages for some very helpful course and career details. You can even download an excellent flow chart which teases out the different specialist routes in the profession. There are also some useful links for anyone wishing to employ particular expertise from a professional psychologist, or to look on the international scene.
★★★   (CLCI: KEL)

Charity Choice   charitychoice.co.uk

Working for charities can be poorly paid, but immensely rewarding. This web site has quite superb links to thousands of charities. The category choice breaks down into nearly 40 main types of charity work from education and community care, to work with the elderly, etc. In many cases you are taken directly to sites of interest and at the very least will then have details to contact regarding employment opportunities.

★★★   (CLCI: KEM)

Charity Commission   charity-commission.gov.uk

The Register of Charities is a fascinating source of information, but perhaps you are considering adding to the present 180,000 charities and need help. Look no further, as this site offers detailed Search and Index pages to assist your research on a wealth of important topics that will need consideration.

★★   (CLCI: KEM)

National Centre for Volunteering   volunteering.org.uk

If you are considering a spell of voluntary work, you will find that this site includes a checklist to help you decide what you may be suited for. You can then look at a number of types of voluntary work and the opportunities available. There are some good tips for those thinking of going overseas, as well as help for organisations that may want to take on volunteers themselves.

★★   (CLCI: KEM)

Voluntary Work   csv.org.uk

This is a great site for anyone prepared to seriously investigate voluntary work. There are hundreds of schemes on offer, as well as help with training for the unemployed or disadvantaged. You can also view current vacancies with CSV from the site map.

★★   (CLCI: KEM)

World Service Enquiry   wse.org.uk

Not for the faint-hearted. You can find anything on this site from summer camps abroad, to being a relief worker overseas, perhaps in very demanding or dangerous situations. However, WSE provides a brilliant online guide to help you prepare for some of the lesser known types of voluntary work overseas.

★★★   (CLCI: KEM)

Other Sites of Interest

Association of Chief Executives of National Voluntary Organisations	**acevo.org.uk**
Barnardo's	**barnardos.org.uk**
British Association for Counselling	**bac.co.uk**
Cafod	**cafod.org.uk/schools.htm**
Camp Counselors (USA)	**campcounselors.com**
Camphill Village Turst	**camphill.org.uk**
Charity Choice Portal	**charitychoice.co.uk**
Charity Jobs	**charityjob.co.uk**
Charity Net	**charitynet.org**
Charity Opportunities	**charityopps.com**
Charity Recruitment	**charec.co.uk**
Childline UK	**childline.org.uk**
Christian Vocations	**christianvocations.org**
International Voluntary Service	**ivsgbn.demon.co.uk**
Leonard Cheshire Foundation	**lcf.org.uk**
National Council of Voluntary Organisations	**ncvo-vol.org.uk**
Northern Ireland Voluntary Trust	**nivt.org**
Occupational Psychology Services	**opsltd.com**
Resources Information Services – Social Inclusion	**ris.org.uk**
The Samaritans	**samaritans.org.uk**
The Scout Association	**scoutbase.org.uk**
Voluntary Development Scotland	**vds.org.uk**
Wales Council for Voluntary Action	**wcva.org.uk**
Worldwide Volunteering	**worldwidevolunteering.org.uk**

ANIMAL HEALTH AND WELFARE

The popular and increasing numbers of animal programmes on television in recent times are likely to have encouraged a greater interest in careers working with animals. However, such interest can often begin with a care and love of pets from an early age; a real concern, almost anger, when seeing them cruelly treated, or even a desire to work outdoors in what for most animals is their natural environment. Animal technicians may not be at the popular end of the industry, but contribute significantly to controlling pests and diseases.

Caring for animals is seldom if ever glamorous. The hours are often long, the work physically tiring, with little prospect of promotion and often low wages. It can be very distressing tending to a wounded animal, hit by a vehicle perhaps, and needing to be put to sleep. You may then find yourself having to comfort the owner, as many jobs with animals often include working with people. However, the rewards are enormous, whether you are maintaining an animal's health and fitness, working a horse up to prime condition for a race meeting, or preventing and treating diseases. Animals are usually totally reliant on their carer and return loyalty and affection in full measure.

Skills and Interests
Listed below are a number of skills, interests and abilities likely to be helpful in working with animals (and, in some cases, their owners!).

- Care, compassion, and love of animals.
- Practical, physically fit and free of allergies.
- Good with people and tactful.
- Patient and dedicated.
- Sensitive and observant.
- Not over-sentimental.
- Science interest.
- Work independently and trustworthy.
- Commercial and business interest.
- Well organised and resourceful.
- Writing, keyboard and communication skills.

Organisations and Work Environment
Zoos, wildlife parks, circuses, animal charities, veterinary practices and hospitals, education and research institutions, commercial fish farms, water authorities, government departments, industrial firms, private estates and angling organisations, hunt and livery stables, racecourses, polo yards, riding schools, trekking and holiday centres, armed forces, breeding, boarding, hunt and racing kennels, guide dog/mobility training centres, pet shops.

The Jobs
Veterinary Surgeon	Veterinary Nurse	Animal Technician
Animal Welfare Inspector	Zookeeper	Fish Farmer

Kennel Worker	Guide Dog Trainer	Dog Groomer
Conservation Park Manager	Pet Shop Assistant	Riding Instructor
Gamekeeper	Horse Groomer	Fisherman
Zoo – work in	Canine Beautician	Cat – work with
Farrier	Groom	Waterkeeper/bailiff

FISH FARMING AND SEA FISHING
CLCI CODES: WAG–WAH

Fish farming is still very much a specialist industry and can be explored further at a number of locations. The Sea Fish Industry Authority site is listed, but check out the imaginative and informative **niseafood.co.uk** which supports the industry in Northern Ireland.

Sea Fish Industry Authority **seafish.co.uk**

Very informative site and a great resource for school projects. There are also some good training pages, although you could easily miss the additional NVW/SVQ details at the foot of the site files section. Includes details of current job vacancies, but little detailed careers information.

 (CLCI: WAH/WAG)

Other Sites of Interest

Fisheries Research Services	**marlab.ac.uk**
Fishing Vessel Course	**lews.uhi.ac.uk**
North Atlantic Fisheries College	**nafc.ac.uk**
Northern Ireland Seafood Ltd	**niseafood.co.uk**

VETERINARY SCIENCE, ANIMAL HEALTH AND WELFARE
CLCI CODES: WAL–WAM

There are some excellent sites to visit among the recommendations below. However, if you have particular interests in an international research centre working to improve the health of farm animals world-wide, then check out **iah.bbsrc.ac.uk**. What better way to plan a visit to the zoo than finding out before you go what is likely to be of particular interest? The 'Who's Who' pages at **edinburghzoo.org.uk** will show you a picture and then give you a brief description of a selection of its animals. You can also explore job pages and voluntary work opportunities. On the domestic scene, if you are interested in puppy breeders and linking them to potential buyers, then **petcare.org.uk** looks to be a useful site.

Association of British Riding Schools   **equiworld.net**

This site is informative, particularly if you are looking for a registered riding school in your region, want a career with horses, or need to find out about all the qualifications available. The links pages are also excellent, with even greater access to anything and everything to do with horses

★★★   (CLCI: WAM)

Battersea Dogs Home   **dogshome.org**

Caring for over 9,000 dogs and cats a year, Battersea Dogs Home is a unique place to work. There are a variety of roles which you can explore further in the about us section of this site, although the actual careers content is quite brief.

★   (CLCI: WAM)

British Horse Society   **bhs.org.uk**

This site has all things equestrian including detailed careers, training and vacancy information. It is also a fun place to surf with interesting links to animation and clip art pages for the real enthusiast to embellish their own web pages.

★★★   (CLCI: WAM)

British Veterinary Nurses Association   **bvna.org.uk**

Aspiring Veterinary Nurses will be encouraged with the pre and post qualifying course information, but will have to research other sources for careers material.

★   (CLCI: WAL)

Chester Zoo   **demon.co.uk/chesterzoo**

Visit Zoo Jobs/Questions for some very good insights, particularly on the different types of careers available in zoos. The information on zookeeping is excellent and I recommend 'A Typical Day in the Life of a Zoo Keeper' as essential reading. The site also includes information on animal care courses.

★★★ (CLCI: WAM)

Royal College of Veterinary Surgeons **rcvs.org.uk**

There is plenty in the visitor pages to encourage the potential veterinary surgeon, with very good careers, education, finance and application pages, including mature and graduate entry for the six universities in Britain that offer courses. However, some caution is advised in relation to the Career Reading list as a number of titles have newer editions.

★★ (CLCI: WAL)

Royal Society for the Protection and Care of Animals **rspca.org.uk**

Good, but limited careers information on careers such as an RSPCA Inspector, veterinary nurses and kennel assistants. However, the Animal Advice pages are excellent and it is a great site for younger children as well as schools looking for curriculum-linked material.

★ (CLCI: WAL)

Vet Web **vetweb.co.uk**

All the pages in this book could not do justice to the amount of information packed into this web site. It is particularly good for the extensive range of links to related animal care. Also includes a useful classified jobs and continual professional development (CPD) section for members, whether you're a vet, nurse, technician or practice manager.

★★ (CLCI: WAL)

Zoological Society, London and Whipsnade Zoos **londonzoo.co.uk**

You will enter London Zoo, Whipsnade and the Zoological Society in one hit. Great fun for exploring the world of animals and conservation for endangered species. The site includes volunteer and work experience opportunities, but you will need to look elsewhere for careers information.

★ (CLCI: WAM)

Other Sites of Interest
Animal Health Trust **aht.org.uk**

Association of British Riding Schools	**abrs.org**
Association of British Wild Animal Keepers	**abwak.co.uk**
Association of Chartered Physiotherapists in Animal Therapy	**acpat.org.uk**
Blue Cross Animal Welfare Charity	**thebluecross.org.uk**
British Horse Racing Board	**bhb.co.uk**
British Veterinary Association	**bva.co.uk**
Department for Environment, Food and Rural Affairs	**defra.gov.uk**
Edinburgh Zoo	**edinburghzoo.org.uk**
Game Conservancy Trust	**game-conservancy.org.uk**
Guide Dogs for the Blind Association	**gdba.org.uk**
Hearing Dogs for Deaf	**hearing-dogs.co.uk**
Horse and Hound Online	**horseandhound.co.uk**
Institute for Animal Health	**iah.bbsrc.ac.uk**
Natural Animal Health	**natural-animal-health.co.uk**
Peoples Dispensary for Sick Animals	**pdsa.org.uk**
Pet Care	**petcare.org.uk**
Scottish Society for the Prevention of Cruelty To Animals	**scottishspca.org**
Society of Practising Veterinary Surgeons	**spvs.org.uk**
Sport Horse Breeding of Great Britain	**sporthorsegb.co.uk**
Support Dog Volunteers	**support-dogs.org.uk**
UK Animal Rescuers	**animalrescuers.co.uk**
Universities Federation for Animal Welfare	**ufaw.org.uk**
Vet Aid	**vetaid.org**
Veterinary Jobs	**vetrecord.co.uk/vetapps.htm**

4
Law, Security
and Protection

Perhaps you're the type of person who is looking for a challenge, but also cares enough to want to make a difference. Careers in law, security and protection services, such as the Armed Forces, are no soft ride or easy option. A barrister or solicitor has to complete a long period of sustained academic study, and then, like the police, develop all the necessary experience and skills to help protect and enforce an individual's or organisation's rights. In reality there are far more students studying law than there are employment vacancies. However, the skills developed during legal training – some of which are listed below – are highly regarded by industry and commerce.

There are over 250,000 men and women who pride themselves upon being among the most professionally trained sailors, soldiers and air-force personnel in the world. Like their colleagues in the fire or coastguard services, they are ready to respond immediately to almost any crisis. Good teamwork is essential and the hours and conditions often extremely unsociable. Yet, ask anyone why they choose such careers and they will say it is because the work is far from routine, it is a great opportunity to keep fit and that the sense of adventure and responsibility in dealing with the unexpected, gives it an edge you just cannot get in other jobs.

Skills and Interests
The following list may be typical of some of the interests you already have, or abilities you would like to develop in a career.

- Desire to serve the community or country.

- Strength of character to deal with difficult situations.

- Sound judgement, mental stamina and intelligence.

- Trustworthy and fair.

- Physical fitness and courage.

- Research and report-writing skills.

- Ability to collect and analyse large amounts of information.
- Weigh up points and counter points.
- Use logical arguments and come to reasoned conclusion based on facts.
- Communicate with clarity.
- Discretion, maturity and patience.
- Good memory.
- Can lead and motivate.

Organisations and Work Environment

Law firms, chambers, criminal courts, advocates' library, commercial companies, prisons, police stations, government departments, local authorities' legal services. Outdoors and in all weathers, commercial and private premises, courts of law, prisons, training units, building sites, vehicles. Sea, air and land operations at home and overseas, training centres hospitals, base ports, air and shore establishments and installations.

The Jobs

Most of the following jobs swear allegiance to the Crown and even wear a uniform, but there the similarities largely end. However, within each career area are many specialist professions, some only possible after a probationary period of training and experience.

Lawyer	Police Constable	Royal Navy Officer
Barrister	Prison Officer	Royal Naval Rating
Legal Executive	Prison Governor	Royal Marine Officer
Research Librarian	Security Officer	Royal Marine
Court Clerk	Fire Officer	Army Officer
Court Officer	Fire-fighter	Army NCO/Private
Traffic Warden	Royal Air Force Officer	Coastguard Officer
Royal Air Force Airman/Airwoman		Detective
Private Investigator		

BARRISTER, SOLICITOR, LEGAL EXECUTIVES AND COURT SERVICES CLCI CODES: L–LAZ

Three cheers for the Internet and **freelawyer.co.uk** and **interactive-lawyer.com** for breaking the mould and encouraging legal information to be more freely available to the public. You are also in for a treat if considering a legal career or wishing to use the web in a professional capacity. There are some excellent sites worthy of research, and it is not just the star-rated ones that have all the best information. Take, for example, **hg.org** which, although it has some US bias, links you directly to a number of useful directories, recommended law firms and lawyers worldwide. Nearer home the Institute of Advanced Legal Studies at **ials.sas.ac.uk** and Inns of Court School of Law **icsl.ac.uk** look very useful for researching academic sites with information about legal training. There is also **biall.org.uk** which represents the interests of all those involved in the crucial research field of law librarianship in Britain and Ireland. Students and aspiring lawyers must delve into **lawlounge.com** for some interesting topics and news features, as well as access to student societies. This section also overlaps with patents and trademarks so **patent.gov.uk** may well be of help complemented by useful advice at **innovation.gov.uk**.

Careers Advisory Network   lcan.csu.ac.uk

Most students in higher education or graduates planning their future will be familiar with this site, which is a major source of information. It is packed with helpful detail on employers, jobs and work experience, career choice and postgraduate opportunities. In this particular case you can explore a number of special law pages on education, training and recruitment, as well as factsheets and good practice guides. There is also excellent advice for students unsuccessful in securing a training contract, who for different reasons may prefer six months paralegal experience, before committing their future to law.

★★★   (CLCI: L)

General Council of the Bar   barcouncil.org.uk

For information on a career as a barrister, look no further than here to start your research. The drop down menu in the qualification pages will set you in the right direction, but do take up the offer to link to the complementary **lawzone.co.uk/barcouncil** site with its comprehensive education and training advice. The link pages from both sites take you on even further points of discovery.

★★★   (CLCI: LAB)

The Institute of Legal Executives   **ilex.org.uk**

You will struggle to find any careers information, but the How to Qualify and Legal Jobs sections are useful.

★   (CLCI: LAD)

Law Careers Net   **lawcareers.net**

This site has everything! It will keep you right up to date with legal news and feature articles. The career pages on becoming a solicitor or barrister are excellent and include helpful advice about A-levels, non-degree entry to law and degree courses and colleges. There are many 'Real Life Case Studies' on a wide variety of careers in law, as well as current trainee and vacation positions to help kick-start your career. If that is not enough, they have even thought to encourage law graduates who may be thinking about alternative careers, recognising the excellent skills that someone who has completed a degree in law has to offer an employer.

★★★   (CLCI: L)

Law Society of England and Wales   **lawsociety.net**

You will find some very good information within 'Qualifying as a Solicitor', but I particularly recommend this site for funding and financial information covering loans, bursaries and sponsorships through law school.

★★   (CLCI: LAC)

Student Law Centre   **studentlaw.com**

You are spoilt for choice as there is little to distinguish this site from Law Careers Net, except perhaps for an excellent CV Do's and Don'ts section and a very helpful page on the qualities that go to make a good barrister. The site map is the place to be if you want to investigate the potential feast before you.

★★★   (CLCI: L)

Other Sites of Interest

Appeals Service	**appeals-service.gov.uk**
Authors' Licensing and Collecting Society	**alcs.co.uk**
Euro Ombudsman	**euro-ombudsman.eu.int**
Bar Council of Northern Ireland	**barcouncil-ni.org.uk**

British and Irish Law Libraries **biall.org.uk**
British Society of
  Criminology **lboro.ac.uk/departments/ss/bcs/homepage/**
Central Applications Board (CPE and LPC courses) **lawcabs.ac.uk**
Council on Tribunals **council-on-tribunals.gov.uk**
Court Services **courtservice.gov.uk**
Crown Prosecution Service **cps.gov.uk**
European Court of Human Rights **echr.coe.int**
Hieros Gamos (comprehensive law and government portal) **hg.org**
Information for Lawyers Ltd **infolaw.co.uk**
Inns of Court School of Law **icsl.ac.uk**
Institute of Patentees and Inventors **invent.org.uk**
International Centre for Commercial Law **icclaw.com**
Internet Lawyer **internetlawyer.com**
Law Lounge **lawlounge.com**
Law Society of Northern Ireland **lawsoc.ni-org**
Law Society of Scotland **lawscot.org.uk**
Legal Resources in UK and Ireland **venables.co.uk**
Northern Circuit Commercial Bar Association **nccba.org.uk**
Northern Ireland Court Services **nics.gov.uk**
Patent and Trade Marks Attorneys **ipr.co.uk**
The Scottish Courts **scotcourts.gov.uk**
Society for Computers in Law **scl.org/welcome**
Society of the Inner Temple **innertemple.org.uk**
UK Patent Office **patent.gov.uk**

POLICE, PRISON, FIRE SERVICE AND SECURITY
CLCI CODES: M–MAZ

You have a good opportunity here to tour all the nation's regional police forces with **police.uk**. They vary in style and presentation, but most constabularies have special recruitment or career pages and other information, which will be very helpful in preparing for interview. The prison service including prison officer, graduate and nursing entry schemes is well represented at the recruitment pages of **hmprisons.gov.uk**. Securicor's site at **securicor.co.uk** and Group 4's at **group4.co.uk** are worth checking out, as they are major UK and international companies and large employers in the security industry.

Fire Net Portal **fire.org.uk**

This site is worthy of mention for its excellent links to just about every fire safety issue, including workplace regulations. On the career front you can reach a new recruitment site, as well as details on fire training establishments. Do also check the companion career pages at **fireservice.co.uk** and other current vacancies listed at **fire-uk.org**.

Government Communications HQ   **gchq.gov.uk**

GCHQ has openings to a wide variety of career positions, including intelligence analysts, linguists, mathematicians and technologists. The career opportunity pages have some useful detail on these and other careers, as well as information on salaries and their special Graduate Management Trainee Scheme. It may be worth exploring some of the vacancies listed as they often give you additional information on working conditions and terms of employment.
★★   (CLCI: MAG)

Maritime and Coastguard Agency   **mcagency.org.uk**

About us, recruitment policy and mca training are the site pages to head for. The news and contact addresses information are also worth noting.
★   (CLCI: MAZ)

Metropolitan Police   **met.police.uk**

This site covers a range of interesting topics, but if you are considering becoming a uniformed police officer then head straight for the excellent recruitment pages. There are also details on the volunteer special constables, which itself is a useful way of testing out a career in the police force, as well as helping in the competitive application process, should you want to go full time. Look out also for other opportunities, as the Met is backed up by an army of support staff, which play a crucial role in fighting crime. Don't leave this site without checking out the index pages, which include links to specialist squads such as Air Support Unit, Mounted Police and Art Squad to name but a few.
★★★   (CLCI: MAB)

Police Service and Recruitment   **police.uk**

The best part of this site is the opportunity to link with police forces throughout the UK. Nearly all constabularies have their own web sites and most include specific recruitment information and details on the Special Constabulary if you're thinking about part-time work. As expected the quality and scope of each site varies, but many have quite detailed information on specialisms with the force such as fraud, firearms, drug prevention or youth liaison work.

★★   (CLCI: MAB)

Other Sites of Interest

City of London Police	**cityoflondon.gov.uk**
Custodial Care national Training Organisation	**ccnto.com**
Fire Service College	**fireservicecollege.ac.uk**
Government Communications HQ	**gchq.gov.uk**
Group4 Security	**group4.co.uk**
HM Prison Service	**hmprisons.gov.uk**
Home Office	**homeoffice.gov.uk**
Interpol	**interpol.com**
Fire Safety Institute	**middlebury.net/firesafe**
The Institution of Fire Engineers	**ife.org.uk**
National Association for the Care & Resettlement of Offenders	**nacro.org.uk**
National Crime Squad	**nationalcrimesquad.police.uk**
National Criminal Intelligence Service	**ncis.co.uk**
Nationwide Investigations Group	**nig.co.uk**
Northern Ireland Prison Service	**niprisonservice.gov.uk**
The Penal Lexicon (Prison and Penal Affairs Subscription Service).	**penlex.org.uk**
Prison Me? No Way!	**pnmw.co.uk**
Prisoners' Education Trust	**prisonerseducation.org**
The Prisoners Handbook	**tphbook.dircon.co.uk**
Royal Ulster Constabulary	**ruc.police.uk**
Scottish Criminal Record Office	**scro.police.uk**
Scottish Prison Service	**sps.gov.uk**
Securicor	**securicor.co.uk**
Security Industry	**sito.co.uk**
Security Companies	**u-net.com/mbp/sol**
UK Fire Services	**fire-uk.org**
Victim Support	**victimsupport.com**

ROYAL NAVY, ARMY, ROYAL AIR FORCE
CLCI CODES: B–BAZ

There is nothing to add to these highly rated sites, except to say that they are clearly in the business of recruiting. Now there are much fewer local Service Career Centres; the web can go some way to bridging the information gap. If you are also interested in international military affairs, then I recommend a look at NATO's site **nato.int**. You could also investigate the Ministry of Defence's link pages **mod.uk** for access to Armed Forces, Ministries and Defence Departments worldwide, as well as other international organisations.

Army	**army.mod.uk**

If you're itching to explore a career in the army, its territorial or cadet forces then look no further. This site is packed with great material, such as checking where in the world the army is currently operating, or exploring the A–Z of regiments and corps. The Equipment pages provide a fascinating glimpse into the type of kit used in modern warfare, including tanks, helicopters and communication systems, and if you are still keen you can even go shopping on-line to buy the T-shirt.

★★★ (CLCI: BAF)

Royal Air Force	**raf.mod.uk**

There is quite an imaginative approach to careers information on this site, as you can use a virtual airbase to select from a range of jobs. The A–Z job search reveals good careers information as well as case study pages of individuals' own stories. You can also have fun testing out your potential interest and skills using an interactive training mission. However, you will need to go back to the official site for more information, including links to RAF squadrons, worldwide operations and a quite useful page on 'Life in the RAF'.

★★★ (CLCI: BAL)

Royal Navy and Royal Marines	**royal-navy.mod.uk**

Make sure you have time to spare on this site, as it is packed with quite amazing detail, colourful images and inspiring messages to make this your chosen career. The RN Jobs pages cover all the careers, entry and training information you need, as well as details on sponsorship for those wishing to be funded through their degree studies. The vital role of the RN and RM Reserves is not forgotten, and another useful option to consider if thirsting for adventure, but also preferring to hold down another job. This is a great site for keeping up with events in the news pages and exploring military history.

★★★ (CLCI: BAB)

Other Sites of Interest

The Air Training Corps	**cranwell.raf.mod.uk**
American Forces Information Service	**defenselink.mil/afis**
British Forces Foundation	**bff.org.uk**
French Foreign Legion	**foreignlegionlife.com**
Ministry of Defence	**mod.uk**
NATO	**nato.int**
Royal Air Forces Association	**rafa.org.uk**
Royal Auxiliary Air Force	**rauxaf.mod.uk**
Royal British Legion – Ex-Servicemen and Women	**rbli.co.uk**
Royal Marines	**royal-marines.mod.uk**

5
Finance, Buying and Selling, Transport and Distribution

The huge predicted growth in business transactions through the Internet may become a reality, but the ultimate success of any modern economy comes down to good management of government fiscal polices, taking account of national and international interests and constraints. This should encourage the right environment for products and services to be manufactured to high standards of quality, which can then be efficiently distributed to the market-place for consumers to buy. However, the backbone to such successes are individuals: people who are stimulated by financial business and being commercially aware. Others perhaps thrive on the challenge to promote their company's image and products through public relations, advertising and marketing. As well as roles in seeking out new and innovative goods and services, there will always be a need for people who enjoy working directly with customers and who take a pride in the skills and service they offer. There are also those roles within the transport industry, that safely moves millions of people every year, who journey on business or pleasure. In addition, the freight industry integrates into the global supply chain to deliver all our material needs.

Skills and Interests
Listed below are a sample of skills and interests which can be particularly appropriate to this sector. Some have a bias towards finance-related occupations, while others apply to many careers.

- Take pleasure in giving customers good service.
- Flair for maths and aptitude for analysing facts and figures.
- Like to be organised.
- Welcome opportunities for travel, perhaps using language skills.
- Diplomatic, honest, reliable.
- Enjoy having responsibility.
- Imaginative and enquiring mind.
- Relish implementing your creative instincts.

- Organisational and communication skills.
- Using high levels of technical knowledge and aptitude.
- Enjoy keeping up to date with commercial and industrial developments.

Organisation and Work Environment – Finance

Private practice, financial institutions, public sector, local authorities, government departments, charities and community organisations, self-employed, international, investment and merchant banks, retail/high street banks, Stock Exchange and building societies.

The Jobs

The following list includes a number of particular careers within finance-related occupations. However, the list is by no means exhaustive (see mathematics in Chapter 6) and a number of the jobs are interchangeable, depending on the type of organisation.

Accountant	Financial Adviser	Taxation Technician
Accounting Technician	Investment Analyst	Tax Inspector
Accounts Clerk	Commodities Broker	Insurance Clerk
Actuary	Market Trader	Insurance Broker
Building Society Manager	Fund Manager	Underwriter
Financial Services Consultant	Loss Adjuster	Stockbroker
Bank Officer	Risk Manager	Internal Auditor
Customer Service Assistant	Bank Manager	Statistician

ACCOUNTANCY, BANKING, INSURANCE AND FINANCIAL SERVICES
CLCI CODES: N–NAZ

You really are spoilt for choice, as there are some high-quality sites on financial careers. Others, however, are excellent on specifics such as **ft.com**'s Career Point pages, where you can match experience you already have, to salary and preferred work location. **bloomberg.com** and **cityjobs.com** are worth a look if you are focusing on the international or city scene for work. However, the real gem for teachers is likely to be the case studies in **pfeg.org.uk**, showing how colleagues are already successfully educating and encouraging the next generation of potential financiers, while at the same time enriching the current curriculum.

Association of Chartered Certified Accountants   **acca.co.uk**

You will find all the normal education and training details within the student pages. There is surprisingly little careers information to suit the first time enquirer and encourage students on this particular route to accountancy. However, the link pages are well worth a visit with access to details on-line accounting journals, as well as excellent range help on job-hunting.

★   (CLCI: NAB)

Association of Accounting Technicians   **aat.co.uk**

If you're the kind of person who is good at and enjoys figure work, but does not want to take the graduate route to financial careers, then this is the place to start your research. The site map will point you to a particularly helpful section called 'Why become an accounting technician?' I also recommend the FAQs and the jobs database, which links you with the complementary **accountingtechnician.co.uk** and offers of help in the studyzone and good careers and job-hunting help.

★★   (CLCI: NAB)

Bank of England   **jobsatthebank.co.uk**

This site is ideal for researching GCSE, A-level and graduate entry routes into working for the Bank of England. Whichever route you take there are helpful personal profiles and learning and development information. You need to enter the 'Interested in Applying' pages to uncover more on the skills needed and the application procedure itself. It is worth noting that you have the option to also visit the main sites home page, which then offers up a treasure trove of useful research material.

★★★   (CLCI: NAD)

Building Societies Association   **bsa.org.uk**

A useful site for keeping up to date with all the changes in building societies changing status to banks. You will find some very helpful careers, education, training and personal profile details within the careers section of the information pages.

★   (CLCI: NAF)

The Chartered Insurance Institute   cii.co.uk

This is a great starting point for taking a first look at careers in insurance. The international pages are worth visiting as more than 11,000 members of the Institute work overseas. The professional qualification and training courses information is well presented, but if you want to investigate an excellent range of employment factsheets drop into the career pages.

★★   (CLCI: NAG)

Chartered Institute of Management Accountants   cima.org.uk

This attractive and informative site is ideally explored through the site map; aspiring accountants will benefit from checking through the prospective students column. Includes details of qualifications, training and careers with helpful FAQ and links pages.

★★★   (CLCI: NAB)

Chartered Institute of Public Finance and Accountancy   cipfa.org.uk

You need to go into the Cipfa vacancy listing pages to locate the comprehensive education and training information. There is much to encourage newcomers as well as experienced accountants within the FAQs and don't miss the site's own listings of current financial jobs, itself a reasonable indicator on the type of salaries one might earn.

★   (CLCI: NAB)

Chartered Institution of Taxation   tax.org.uk

Don't be put off by the opening credits on this movie as the site map and inserting careers in the search facility will take you to some useful information including 'Considering Careers in Business and Finance?' Then, I'm afraid it's back to the site map for student and excellent help on exam techniques.

★★   (CLCI: NAK)

Institute of Chartered Accountants   icaew.co.uk

About Chartered Accountancy listed in the home page is as good a place as any to start your search, whether a new or a seasoned professional. It includes links to a helpful FAQs section. However, potential or new students will also benefit from dropping into the student and training section, with 'how to become a chartered accountant' then taking you through to the accounting technician, A-level and graduate routes to being qualified. Also, don't miss the trainee vacancy and further information details.

★★★ (CLCI: NAB)

Institute of Financial Services cib.org.uk

Head straight for the career development and career management services pages for some helpful information, some of which can be downloaded. Not the easiest site thereafter to navigate and much of the material seems to have a price tag.

★ (CLCI: NAD)

PricewaterhouseCoopers pwcglobal.com/uk

PricewaterhouseCoopers are among the country's leading management consultants. This is a great site for keeping in touch with the world of international business and finance. There are also very good pages for graduates or undergraduates on anything from summer vacation placements to gap year, work shadowing and current employment opportunities. Sixth Formers and Gap Year students have an opportunity to put their skills to the test and try out a pre-university interactive quiz.

★★ (CLCI: N)

The Securities Institute securities-institute.org.uk

If a financial career in the City of London interests you, then you will like this site. The site map points to careers and an excellent range of city finance careers. Check out job profiles, which vary from brief comments to complete 'day in the life' stories. I particularly recommend the Hints and Tips pages which will help with job-hunting in this competitive sector. You can also get good information from the link pages which apparently the professionals themselves use.

★★ (CLCI: NAK)

Other Sites of Interest

Accountancy Tutors	**atew.com**
Association of British Insurers	**abi.org.uk**
Association of Unit Trusts and Investment Funds	**investmentfunds.org.uk**

Bloomberg	**bloomberg.com**
British Bankers Association	**bba.org.uk**
European Central Bank	**ecb.int**
Financial Information Net Directory	**find.co.uk**
Financial Services Authority	**fsa.gov.uk**
Financial Times	**ft.com**
Institute of Chartered Accountants of Scotland	**icas.org.uk**
Institute of Public Finance	**ipf.co.uk**
Institute of Revenues Rating and Valuation	**irrv.org.uk**
International Monetary Fund	**imf.org**
KPMG	**kpmg.co.uk**
London International Financial Futures.	**liffe.com**
London Stock Exchange	**londonstockexchange.com**
Personal Finance Education Group	**pfeg.org.uk**
Treasury Office	**hm-treasury.gov.uk**

Organisation and Work Environment – Buying and Selling

Marketing and advertising agencies, retail and specialist shops and chain stores, public relations consultancies, in-house PR departments, warehouses, salons, beauty clinics and modelling agencies.

The Jobs

Listed below are some of the main types of work that can be found in this sector. Some of the jobs are interchangeable between different organisations.

Marketing and Advertising	Buying and Selling	Buyer
Advertising Executive	Bookseller	Art Dealer
Media Executive	Builder's Merchant	Sales Manager
Press Officer	Retailer	Carpet Fitter
Bill Poster	Butcher	Sales Assistant
Classified Advertising Sales	Agricultural Supplier	Florist
Marketing Consultant	Sales Representative	Car Salesperson
Copywriter	Store Demonstrator	Fishmonger
PR Consultant	Customer Services	Wholesaler
Conference Organiser	Cobbler	Licensed Trade
Market Researcher	Technical Sales	Telephone Sales
Modelling	Call Centre Manager	Telesales Assistant

MARKETING, ADVERTISING AND MEDIA
CLCI CODES: O–OD

Good independent research is recognised as being essential to the success of most global companies. International Research Institutes at **iris-net.org** may well help you to implement strategic changes to continue such success and perhaps secure new markets for the future. If media appeals then you cannot go far wrong with **mediavillage.co.uk** The links pages alone will connect you to over 2,500 UK and international media sites. Media buffs will also be impressed with the specialist recruitment portal for media sales and marketing work at **mediacareer.co.uk**. The site provides a useful daily summary of current vacancies by job title. Demand is outstripping supply in technically creative jobs such as those related to electronic media. So, if you have relevant postgraduate qualifications or two years' employment experience, then **recruitmedia.co.uk** is well worth a visit, with its impressive vacancy listing including permanent, freelance and executive positions. It perhaps comes as no surprise that the Telesales and Call Centre business are among the UK's fastest growing industries. **telepeople.com** will keep you well up to date with vacancies. However, also have an eye to the future as IT developments suggest potential openings for contract work from home.

Advertising Association	adassoc.org.uk

The links pages could keep anyone researching advertising busy for hours, but the Information Centre is where you need to be for excellent insights into this very competitive profession. There are some very helpful student briefing papers, and the full text of the 'Getting into Advertising: A Careers Guide' includes useful tips on qualifications and job-hunting.

★★★ (CLCI: OD)

Chartered Institute of Marketing	cim.co.uk

You may not need to look much further than this excellent site if you are considering a career in marketing, or even looking to develop your skills and experience within the industry. The careers and development, qualification and training pages are packed with helpful advice. You can access a number of specialist recruitment agency web sites. Members can use the institute's own career counselling advisers and job search service, but some sample vacancies can be viewed within job focus, although most of the vacancies listed are likely to interest those already well established in the profession.

★★★ (CLCI: OD)

Institute of Practitioners in Advertising **ipa.co.uk**

This site received a three-star rating when last reviewed, but unfortunately the contents, including career pages, are only available by registering your details.

★ (CLCI: OD)

MORI (Market Opinion Research International) **mori.com**

Check the newly created and informative carrers pages if you're interested in being a researcher. Perhaps you already possess some of the specialist knowledge and skills they require.

★★ (CLCI: O)

Other Sites of Interest

Advertising Age (USA)	**adage.com**
The Communications Advertising and Marketing Educational Foundation	**camfoundation.com**
Incorporated Society of British Advertisers	**isba.org.uk**
International Research Institutes	**iris-net.org**
Marketing & Advertising Recruitment	**emrsearch.co.uk**
Media Career Vacancies	**mediacareer.co.uk**
Media Village	**mediavillage.co.uk**
Mintel Marketing Intelligence	**mintel.co.uk**
Office of Fair Trading	**oft.gov.uk**
Recruitmedia	**recruitmedia.co.uk**

RETAILING, PUBLIC RELATIONS, BUYING AND MODELLING
CLCI CODES: OE–OZ

If you are interested in a career in retailing, take a look at a number of familiar brand names who are now hosting career pages and vacancy information on their web sites, including **j-sainsbury.co.uk**, **clarks.com**, **marksandspencer.com**, **johnlewis.co.uk** and **asda.co.uk**. When it comes to recruiting within the retail sector, there are few to match the services provided by **rhr.co.uk**. There will always be sites with little or no careers information, but it is still important to check them out. **icas.co.uk** is a good example of a site which, although an independent public relations agency, hosts links to trade journals and international agencies. **prschool-london.com** may also be worth visiting, particularly if you are prepared to do a 15-week evening course to assimilate all the basics of practical PR work. If you have a business and are looking to export for the first time, **export.co.uk** will give you all the help you need to register your company, as well as provide access to the British Exporters Database, should you wish to purchase products and services. Getting started with a career in modelling must be difficult at the best of times but **models.co.uk** is a good place to begin, as there is plenty of advice, as well as agencies you might approach. Fashion Net at **fashion.net** also includes modelling information. You should also check out the fashion and clothing sites (Chapter 2), since a number include references to careers in beauty and modelling.

Brewers and Licensed Retailers Association   **blra.co.uk**

This is a superb site with everything you need to know about careers in licensed retailing, brewing, running a pub and much more besides. Qualifications are also well covered and there are further contacts and web sites to help your research.

★★★   (CLCI: OFM)

The Chartered Institute of Purchasing and Supply   **cips.org**

This site is rated more for its qualifications and training details than its limited information on careers. The vacancy pages look useful and you can find an impressive international listing of other purchasing and supply management organisations from the site's external links.

★   (CLCI: OP/OM)

The Institute of Export   **export.org.uk**

This is mainly designed for members of the Institute, and has attractive features such as the 'Discussion Forum' where professionals can share ideas and experiences. However, there is useful information within 'Education and Training' on professional qualifications, continuing professional development and opportunities for home study. Includes own recruitment portal.

★   (CLCI: OM)

Institute of Public Relations	**ipr.org.uk**

This site has trebled its star rating with its very informative Careers in PR and Career Development Guide which covers a range of course options in universities and colleges. The Training information is useful if you are looking towards IPR Foundation and Diploma courses and the PR Job Shop includes vacancies at officer, manager and executive level.

★★★   (CLCI: OG)

Other Sites of Interest

Asda	**asda.co.uk**
Body Shop	**the-body-shop.com**
Bookselling	**thebookseller.com**
British Footwear Association	**britfoot.com**
Clarks Shoes	**clarks.com**
Coca-Cola (US)	**cocacola.com**
Exhibitions – NEC, etc.	**necgroup.co.uk**
Fashion Net	**fashion.net**
Institute of Grocery Distribution	**igd.com**
John Lewis Partnership	**johnlewis.co.uk**
Leather	**leathernet.com**
Marks and Spencer	**marks-and-spencer.co.uk**
Modelling – Getting Discovered (USA)	**supermodel.com/aspire**
Next	**next.co.uk**
Online Learning Resources	**di-net.co.uk**
Public Relations Agency	**icas.co.uk**
Public Relations Consultants Association	**prca.org.uk**
Retail Human Resources plc	**rhr.co.uk**
Sainsbury	**j-sainsbury.co.uk**
Source of Supply (UK) Ltd	**export.co.uk**
Super Net Models	**supernetmodels.com**
Tesco	**tesco.co.uk**
Trade Partners UK	**tradepartners.gov.uk**
UK Warehousing Association	**ukwa.org.uk**

Organisation and Work Environment – Transport and Distribution

Airports, air traffic control centres, aircraft and maintenance hangars, road and rail companies, traffic offices, passenger and freight vehicles, trains, railway stations, track lines, workshops and regional signal centres, merchant and cruise ships, ferries and tug boats, ports and inland waterways, chartering and freight forwarding companies, postal sorting offices and mailing agencies.

The Jobs

Below are examples of work that can be found in this sector. Most are listed for their broad or direct relation to transport. However, as many of the jobs are also associated with engineering and manufacturing, it will be helpful to investigate the relevant sections in Chapter 6.

Air Cabin Crew	Canal Work	Chauffeur
Civil Pilot	Lock Keeper	Van Driver
Air Traffic Controller	Deck Officer	Lorry Driver
Flight Engineer	Docker	Forklift Truck Driver
Air Broker	Ship Broker	Forklift Truck Mechanic
Airline Administration	Freight Forwarder	Bus Driver / Conductor
Astronaut	Deck Hand	Coach Driver
Passenger Service	Harbour Work	Road Safety Officer
Steward	Hovercraft Work	Distribution Manager
Helicopter Pilot	Sea Cabin Crew	Transport Planner
Air Maintenance	Navigating Officer	Driving Instructor
Airport Manager	Purser	Train Driver
Radio Officer	Signalman / Woman	Rail Engineer
Sailor	Ticket Collector	Furniture Removals
Postman / Woman		

AIR, ROAD, RAIL, SEA TRANSPORT AND LOGISTICS
CLCI CODES: Y–YAZ

A student, job applicant or business manager can find plenty of interest on **transportweb.com** which includes a list of training courses as well as an amazing link to UK and international transport industry web sites. For public consumption **pti.org.uk** is well worth a visit as it is a very good Transport Information Service, again with excellent links to other major transport organisations. Perhaps you're keen to prepare well for an interview and want to be more aware of government policies or national issues affecting the transport industry. You will find a wealth of material at the Department of the Environment, Transport and the Regions site at **detr.gov.uk**. If you are looking towards MSc, PG Dip, BA/BSc and NVQ/SVQs courses then check out the Institution of High-ways and Transportation's excellent Professional Development pages at **iht.org**. A great site for maps and directions is **multimap.com**.

As one may expect, **virgin.com** is a highly imaginative and presenta-ble site packed with travel, retail and recruitment information across an impressive empire. There are also real gems such as Virgin Cosmetics and the opportunity to be an independent consultant in partnership with Sir Richard Branson. The increased number of flights in and out of the UK always seems to be in the news. You can gen up on the official line from the Civil Aviation Authority at **nats.co.uk** as well as visit their recruitment information.

The web (and especially **rail.co.uk**) is ideal for keeping up to speed on railway travel routes, ticket information and offers by all the major train operators, including special services to Disneyland near Paris or skiing in the French Alps. However, you will have to search hard for careers information and in most cases it is advisable to write directly to the contact addresses. Graduates could also check out Railtrack below and perhaps GT Railway Maintenance at **gtrm.com**.

The British International Freight Association at **bifa.org** includes some exciting new distance learning courses, and other useful educational, training and link pages. They are keen to close the skills gap in the industry, but there is little sign of careers information and job vacancies. If thinking internationally then it will be worth visiting **freightnet.com**. A further site particularly for small businesses looking to distribute their goods is **andys-now2business.co.uk**.

British Airways   britishairwaysjobs.com

Very impressive careers pages and recruitment information await you at British Airways. There are details on a wide range of employment possibilities whether you are a graduate, potential pilot or engineer, interested in cabin crew, or in supporting worldwide cargo operations. Don't miss the FAQs and there are some very helpful tips on preparing your CV. The world's largest airline is living up to its name.
★★★   (CLCI: YAB)

British Ports Industry Training   bpit.co.uk

There is just so much that is noteworthy about this site. The career pages are very helpful with an opportunity to explore a wide range of job types that support this crucial industry. The link pages are probably of equal interest to the geography student, as details on most of the world's largest ports are listed. If looking for work, don't miss the current vacancy details and an excellent employer's map locator.
★★★   (CLCI: YAG)

Chamber of Shipping   **british-shipping.org**

This site provides a useful glimpse into a life in the merchant navy (also see Ship Safe Training below). The training and careers pages are your port of call with helpful advice on entrance requirements, employment prospects and training, plus links to the maritime colleges. There are useful education pages, which may also appeal to Teachers. The FAQs give details if you fancy paying your passage on a cargo vessel to almost any of the main trade destinations in the world.

★★   (CLCI: YAL)

The Institute of Logistics and Transport   **iolt.org.uk**

This is well worth visiting for masses of good careers information and advice. There are also helpful pages on education and training, including short courses in logistics and opportunities for continuing professional development. The researcher as much as career applicant will benefit from the extensive links to associated web sites.

★★   (CLCI: Y)

Maritime and Coastguard Agency   **mcagency.org.uk**

The About us recruitment policy and mca training are the site pages to head for. The news and contact addresses information are also worth noting. The press releases make fascinating reading.

★   (CLCI: YAL)

Merchant Navy Training Board   **mntb.org.uk**

Although some of this site was under development at the time of writing, there is still some excellent information within the careers, training and sponsorship pages. Also, plenty of additional facts and figures on the industry and life at sea that some readers are sure to want to gain their 'sea legs'!

★★   (CLCL: YAL)

Rail Industry   **ritc.org.uk**

This is a high-quality informative site on a wide range of career opportunities within the rail industry. Look out for the excellent career path summaries, qualification finder service and recruitment pages.

★★★   (CLCI: YAF)

Railtrack	**railtrack.co.uk**

This site is particularly suitable for graduates seeking a career in the rail industry. There are opportunities from any degree discipline, as well as the more specific, such as civil engineering, electrical, electronic and mechanical engineering. Includes very brief employment profiles, training and development information and vacancies. Important to keep in touch with main graduate recruitment dates which normally begin in September.

★★ (CLCI: YAF)

Ship Safe Training Group	**sstg.org**

This is almost a companion site to the Chamber of Shipping, as the Ship Safe Training Group select and train officer cadets and personnel for over 300 merchant and cruise vessels. The details are quite brief but represent a useful starting point.

★ (CLCI: YAL)

Other Sites of Interest

Air Traffic Control	**nats.co.uk**
Automobile Association	**theaa.co.uk**
Big Blue – A Passion for Boating	**bigblue.org.uk**
British Airline Pilots Association	**balpa.org.uk**
British International Freight Association	**bifa.org**
British Marine Equipment Council	**bmec.org.uk**
British Motorcyclists Federation	**bmf.co.uk**
British National Space Centre	**bnsc.gov.uk**
British Sub-Aqua Club	**bsac.com**
Brittany Ferries	**brittany-ferries.com**
Caledonian MacBrayne	**calmac.co.uk**
Chartered Institute of Transport	**citrans.org.uk**
Civil Aviation Authority	**caa.co.uk**
Department of the Environment, Transport and the Regions	**detr.gov.uk**
Distributive National Training Organisation	**dnto.com**
Dive International	**dive-international.net**
Diving for Women	**womeninscuba.com**
Driving Services	**drivingservices.com**
English, Welsh and Scottish Railway (Freight)	**ews-railway.co.uk**
European Local Transport Information Service	**eltis.org**
Eurostar	**eurostar.com**
Fred Olsen	**fredolsen.co.uk**

Freight Forward International Limited	**freightnet.com**
Freight Transport Association	**fta.co.uk**
GT Railway Maintenance	**gtrm.com**
Guild of Air Traffic Controllers	**gatco.org**
Inland Waterways Association	**waterways.org.uk**
Institution of Highways and Transportation	**iht.org**
London Transport	**londontransport.co.uk**
London Underground	**thetube.com**
Maritime and Coastguard Agency	**mcga.gov.uk**
Motor Careers	**motor-careers.co.uk**
Motor Industry Training Council	**mitc.co.uk**
National Sea Training Centre	**nwkent.ac.uk/nstc**
National Union of Maritime Aviation and Shipping Transport	**numast.org**
National Union of Rail, Maritime and Transport Workers	**rmt.org.uk**
Office of the Rail Regulator	**rail-reg.gov.uk**
Online Learning Resources	**di-net.co.uk**
Passenger Transport National Training Organisation	**transfed.org**
P & O Ferries	**pogroup.com**
Public Transport Information	**pti.org.uk**
RAC	**rac.co.uk**
Railway Industry	**ritc.org.uk**
Road Haulage National Training Organisation	**rhdtc.co.uk**
Royal Mail	**royalmail.com**
Sail Links	**sailinks.co.uk**
Sailing Opportunities	**sunsail.com**
SeaNet – Maritime Services	**seanet.co.uk**
Securicor	**securicor.co.uk**
SFT Aviation	**sft.co.uk**
TNT	**tnt.co.uk**
The Transport Web	**transportweb.com**
UK Hydrographic Office	**ukho.gov.uk**
UK Railways	**rail.co.uk**
UK Diving Resource	**ukdiving.co.uk**
United Road Transport Union	**urtu.com**
Virgin	**virgin.com**

6
Science, Manufacturing, Construction and Land Use

Exciting, amazing, challenging, even daunting are just a few of the words that help sum up the effects of recent scientific and technological advances on our lives, let alone the new frontiers we are about to explore. Who would have imagined a few years ago the influence of electronics and miniaturisation: from mobile phones and laptop communicating across the globe, to the use of robotics in manufacturing? What about the so-called 'smart' homes of the future, which will predict and respond to particular requirements such as ordering your shopping automatically? In addition, there have been incredible advances in medical science, helping to eradicate once life-threatening diseases, as well as increasing general life expectancy. At the root of such success are often dedicated scientists and engineers, the unsung heroes in laboratories and research centres. However, new challenges remain for even our most basic needs, such as how to make the best and healthiest use of land, water and energy resources to sustain a huge increase in the world's population in this new century.

Skills and Interests
Listed below are a sample of personal qualities, skills and interests that can be found among the science, technology or land-based industries. Such attributes can often indicate suitability to particular careers and so are perhaps worthy of further investigation.

- Keen interest in subjects like maths, physics, chemistry and biology.
- Good at communicating ideas and theories.
- Enjoy being methodical and accurate with attention to detail.
- Like to work with figures and analysing data.
- An interest in craft, design and technology.
- Good technical knowledge.
- Concern for the countryside, wildlife conservation and the environment.

- Interest in business, organisations and management.
- Like practical work, being outdoors and involved in nature.
- Adaptable and flexible.
- Patient and persistent with good powers of observation.
- Have an enquiring and logical mind.
- Enjoy working independently.
- Have a creative and practical approach to problem solving.

Organisations and Work Environment – Science and Manufacturing
Laboratories, specialist retail shops, offices, educational institutions, research centres, hospitals, private clinics and health centres, factories, workshops and assembly lines, industrial plants, land and offshore installations, weather centres, building sites, garages, private homes.

SCIENCE
CLCI CODES: Q–QOZ

The Jobs
Listed below are a number of science and mathematics related jobs. If you have a keen interest in sciences and possibly a career using such subjects as physics, biology and chemistry, then this section should also be viewed alongside careers in health and medical professions, engineering and manufacturing.

Agricultural Surveyor

Biologist	Chemist	Laboratory Assistant
Botanist	Colour Scientist	Scientific Officer
Biotechnologist	Pharmacologist	Food Scientist
Ornithologist	Forensic Scientist	Economist
Geneticist	Soil Scientist	Cosmetic Scientist
Marine Biologist	School Technician	Metallurgist
Zoologist	Astronomer	Environmental Scientist
Ecologist	Meteorologist	Oceanographer
Marine Geologist	Weather Forecaster	Mathematician
Statistician	Physicist	Biochemist

If you are a scientist and want to keep up to date with informed topical opinion on current issues, you must visit **nature.com**. The daily science update service is quite a feature of this site. There are also very helpful details on fellowships, studentships and scholarship awards, and if job-hunting on the international scene you will find much of interest across a wide range of science professions. It is refreshing to find a site such as **set4women.gov.uk** dedicated to promoting opportunities for women to enter careers in science, engineering and technology. It will be of interest to school and college students, as well as to women returners, with advice on free or low-cost courses to help bring your valuable knowledge up to date. Should economics be your interest, then you will want to check on the Institute of Economic Affairs at **iea.org.uk**. It seems mainly about membership and promoting half-price book sales to students, but look for the link page on 'Think Tanks' which includes UK, European, US and other international groups. Environmental Data Services at **ends.co.uk** has been producing environmental intelligence for the professionals for over 20 years. This is a great site if you want to view their European environmental news service, look for environmental jobs, or access the very useful Environmental Consultants Directory.

British Ecological Society   **demon.co.uk/bes**

Do not be put off by the rather bland presentation of this site. If you have an interest in ecology, you need look no further. From the news section you can access the full 36-page text of the society's new booklet *Careers in Ecology and Environmental Management*, which is just packed with the best insights and advice you can get, including associated web sites and job-hunting help.

★★★   (CLCI: QOD/QOL)

British Pharmacological Society   **bps.ac.uk**

From links to the European Pharmacology Network, a range of specialist job-hunting agencies as well as educational resources for schools, this site has it all. There is some excellent information on drugs and other topics related to the wider industry, including superb links to companies' own web sites. However, the real jewel is 'Careers in Pharmacology', which will stimulate any aspiring scientist to take a closer look at this important health industry.

★★★   (CLCI: QOB)

Business and Economics on the Internet   **bized.ac.uk**

This is a brilliant resource for sixth-form or undergraduate students studying business or economics. You can browse an extensive Business

Internet catalogue, and link to the FTSE 100 top companies in the UK and their web sites, which you can use to seek out opportunities for employment. You can even download virtual company and economy packages to help with projects, and there are also some very useful tips on study skills.

★★   (CLCI: QOK)

Defence Evaluation and Research Agency   **dera.gov.uk**

You simply must visit the Graduate Recruitment section to see the amazing range of careers that can open up for you. DERA employs the largest community of scientists and engineers in Europe, and you can discover some of the fascinating projects undertaken by checking out the case-study pages. If you are serious about working for the organisation, there is plenty of advice and help, including a list of current vacancies.

★★★   (CLCI: Q)

Forensic Science Service   **forensic.gov.uk**

The careers and forensic careers links offer useful advice for students thinking about university, including a list of recommended related science courses. Unfortunately, there is very little on careers, but the FAQs do answer most questions. They are further complemented by the Case Files tucked into the news pages, which are great if you want to find out a little more about the success of forensic science and the impact that new advances in DNA are making in criminal investigations.

★★   (CLCI: QOT)

Geological Society   **geolsoc.org.uk**

The careers section is excellent on this site. It covers education and training, as well as continual professional development information for existing employees. A wide range of associated organisations can be accessed off the Directories page.

★★   (CLCI: QOL)

Institute of Food Science and Technology   **ifst.org**

You do not need to be an aspiring food scientist to enjoy this site. The FAQs and associated web links are fascinating and there is masses of useful content for researchers to delve into. However, although there are useful course and qualification details, the lack of careers information is disappointing.

★ (CLCI: QON)

Institute of Materials   **instmat.co.uk**

Few will be aware of the tremendous employment opportunities in following a career as a materials scientist. This site introduces the profession within the career pages, which also link you to the hugely helpful **materials-careers.org.uk**. Also check out the informative Student and Education part of the site covering details on salaries, sponsorships and accredited courses and a special younger members section. However, if you want to get genned up for an interview and be well versed in current issues, then you simply must visit the *Materials World Journal* located in the site map; use the links for an international perspective on the profession, and look out for the 'jobs in materials' page for current vacancies.

★★★ (CLCI: QOS)

Institute of Physics   **iop.org**

If you're interested in physics then this is a great site to explore. You need to check the on-line services section to find the latest vacancies or 'Physics for...' to explore educational resources for schools and colleges. Students can join a discussion forum around the globe and look for summer placement opportunities. However, it seems you have to contact the Institute direct for careers information.

★ (CLCI: QOF)

The Met Office   **met-office.gov.uk**

Yes, you can find out the latest weather forecast – and not just in the United Kingdom, as there are some excellent links to international weather stations. The ideal place to start your careers research is from the education and then the About and Learn sections listed at the index.

★★ (CLCI: QOL)

Oceanography   **soc.soton.ac.uk**

This site is hosted by the University of Southampton's Oceanography Centre. You will find much of interest, but need to visit the Information for Schools pages for career gems and search facility on jobs for other useful material.

★★ (CLCI: QOL)

Royal Society of Chemistry   chemsoc.org

Head for the careers and job centre for just about all your needs. As well as finding current job vacancies, you can also get help writing your CV, or preparing for interviews. The careers information is good providing you already know what area of chemistry you're interested in. However, if you are concerned about mid to late career issues then visit the professional chemist's toolkit, which includes an excellent series of topical career features. The educational arcade is also well worth checking out and likely to be of interest to teachers as well as potential students and scientists.

★★★ (CLCI: QOB)

Society for General Microbiology   socgenmicrobiol.org.uk

Follow the education and careers pages and you're into a wealth of excellent material that will greatly encourage your research. The careers information is very good with help on courses and qualifications, as well as the types of skills and qualities required to be a microbiologist. You can keep up to date with the latest issues by visiting journals. Then there are the link pages if you want to get a greater feel for the profession, not least on the international scene.

★★★ (CLCI: QOD)

Other Sites of Interest

A Level Tutorials, Exercises and Tests	**mathsdirect.co.uk**
Association for Science Education	**ase.org.uk**
Association of the British Pharmaceutical Industry	**abpi.org.uk**
Biochemical Society	**biochemsoc.org.uk**
Biotechnology and Biological Sciences Research Council	**bbsrc.ac.uk**
British Geological Survey	**bgs.ac.uk**
British Society of Immunology	**immunology.org**
Economist	**economist.co.uk**
Electronics, Engineering, Plastics and Rubber	**apgate.com**
Environmental Data Services Ltd	**ends.co.uk**
Example – University Meteorology Course	**met.rdg.ac.uk**
Forensic Science Society	**forensic-science-society.org.uk**
Forensics	**sol.co.uk/pfsld**

Gateway to Chemical Industry	**sourcerer.co.uk**
Geography Information Gateway	**geog.le.ac.uk/cti/info.html**
Government Economics Service	**ges.gov.uk**
ICL	**icl.com**
Institute of Biology	**iob.org**
Institute of Biomedical Sciences	**ibms.org**
Institute of Economic Affairs	**iea.org.uk**
Institute of Mathematics and its Applications	**ima.org.uk**
Institute of Physics and Engineering in Medicine	**ipem.org.uk**
Institute of Science and Technology	**istonline.org**
Institute of Scientific and Technical Communications	**istc.org.uk**
Institution of Chemical Engineers	**whynotchemeng.com**
The London Mathematical Society	**lms.ac.uk**
Mathematical Association	**m-a.org.uk**
Maths At Work Project	**mathsatwork.com**
MathSphere	**mathsphere.co.uk**
The Meteorological Office	**met-office.gov.uk**
National Endowment for Science Technology and the Arts	**nesta.org.uk**
National Geographic	**nationalgeographic.com**
National Statistics	**statistics.gov.uk**
The National Training Centre	**forensic-training.police/uk**
Natural Environment Research Council	**nerc.ac.uk**
New Scientist Careers	**newscientist.com/graduate**
Pharmaceutical, Biotechology and Healthcare Jobs	**pharmavacancies.com**
Physics and Astronomy	**pparc.ac.uk**
Renowned Geography Fieldwork Centre	**weymouth.gov.uk/case4inx.htm**
Royal Botanic Gardens	**rbgkew.org.uk**
Royal Geographical Society	**rgs.org**
Royal Statistical Society	**rss.org.uk**
Science in Action	**bbc.co.uk/sia**
Science Museum	**sciencemuseum.org.uk**
Science Net	**sciencenet.org.uk**
Science Resources	**sciquest.com**
Science Technician Vacancies	**young-scientist.co.uk**
Science Technology and Mathematics Council	**stmc.org.uk**
Society for Underwater Technology	**sut.org.uk**
Society of Business Economists	**sbe.co.uk**
Southampton Oceanography Centre	**soc.soton.ac.uk**
Tech Jobs	**techjobs.co.uk**
UK and International Science Vacancies	**nature.com**

UK Location Map   **multimap.com**
Women in Science, Engineering and Technology   **set4women.gov.uk**

ENGINEERING AND MANUFACTURING
CLCI CODES: R–SOZ

The Jobs

Aeronautical Engineer	Agricultural Engineer	Baker
Antique Furniture Restorer	Assembly Worker	Vehicle Mechanic
Forklift Truck Mechanic	Naval Architect	Blacksmith
Recording Engineer	Automobile Engineer	Tailor
Welder	Vehicle Body Repairer	Brewer
Boat Builder	Watch/Clock Repairer	Typesetter
Biomedical Engineer	Chemical Engineer	Woodworker
Bus/Coach Repairer	Tyre and Exhaust Fitter	Shoe Repairer
Broadcast Engineer	Building Engineer	Dressmaker
Coal Miner	Electrician	Factory Worker
Mining Engineer	Production Engineer	Machinist
Marine Engineer	Mechanical Engineer	Locksmith
Musical Instrument Repairer	Farm Mechanic	Piano Tuner
Electrical Engineer	Photographic Processor	Offshore Worker
Electronic Engineer	Gas Engineer	Print Operator

The Society of British Aerospace Companies site at **sbac.co.uk** will keep you well informed on Farnborough International Air Shows, but what really caught my eye were the amazing products and services pages. An A–Z listing identifies just about every manufactured product in the industry and then links you to the appropriate Directory of Members, many with their own web sites. Your next stop might well be the Institution of Mechanical Engineers at **imeche.org.uk** which includes a useful introduction to this specialist branch of the engineering profession. A Young Members' site was under construction at time of going to print, but something worthy of recommendation is the links page which boasts an excellent array of related industries. It may be hard to imagine, but the Builders Merchants Federation sells over £6.2 billion of building materials to the trade and public each year.

British Coatings Federation (NTO)   **coatings.org.uk**

Short on careers information, but excellent on training and qualifications for entering the industry. For example, GNVQ/NVQ/SNVQ are all well covered, but mature entrants will be particularly encouraged with the 'Open Tech Online' pages. If you are looking for anything about decorative coatings, industrial coatings and printing inks, then look no further than the information and at website link.

★ (CLCI: SAV)

British Helicopter Advisory Board   bhab.demon.co.uk

Aspiring helicopter pilots and engineers will be delighted with this site, as it provides all the essential information required to enter this specialist field of civil aviation. The index pages reveal a wealth of interesting features related to the wider industry, from gaining local authority low-flying planning consent, to building your own helipad.

★★ (CLCI: RAC)

British National Space Centre   bnsc.gov.uk

What this site may lack in presentation, it makes up for in providing access to a wide range of information on the space industry. A little cumbersome using the indexes but the Space Jobs pages provide a fascinating glimpse into the types of international careers that one would never normally hear about.

★ (CLCI: RAC)

Countryside Agency   countryside.gov.uk

An impressive site by any standards, with masses of information on the environment, transportation and conservation. Visit the reception area for current job information and Our work to get a real feel for the issues in the rural economy.

★★ (CLCI: SAW)

Defence Evaluation and Research Agency   dera.gov.uk

You simply must visit the Graduate Recruitment section to see the amazing range of careers that can open for you. DERA employ the largest community of scientists and engineers in Europe, and you can discover some of the fascinating projects undertaken by checking out the case study pages. If you are serious about securing work with the organisation, there is plenty of advice and help, including a list of current vacancies.

★★★ (CLCI: R)

Engineering and Marine Training Authority   **emta.org.uk**

Brilliant! This has to be one of the most informative and enjoyable introductions to the world of engineering. You can explore through the complementary enginuity link pages a number of themes including inside engineering, behind the scenes and getting there. The site is just packed with useful information, which will be of equal interest to young people, non-scientists and mature students. The 'get a life' quiz is also fun, but don't miss the opportunity to explore the many facets of engineering offered in the enginuity pages.

★★★   (CLCI: R)

The Federation of Bakers   **bakersfederation.org.uk**

This site's careers pages are very informative on a wide range of related jobs in the baking industry. Also, details on the right qualifications to pursue. From the 'industry facts' pages you can explore an impressive list of companies which have their own web sites. Not a bad idea if you are looking for work, as the Federation of Bakers produces 80% of the nation's bread and has a turnover of over £2 billion.

★★   (CLCI: SAC)

Government Communications HQ   **gchq.gov.uk**

GCHQ has openings to a wide variety of career positions, including intelligence analysts, linguists, mathematicians and technologists. The careers opportunity pages have some useful detail on these and other careers, as well as information on salaries and their special Graduate Management Trainee Scheme. It may be worth exploring some of the vacancies listed, as they often give you additional information on working conditions and terms of employment.

★★   (CLCI: R)

Institute of Marine Engineers   **imare.org.uk**

Amazing site. You could spend hours here, but I recommend a visit first to the 'careers in maritime engineering' details located from the recruitment and then career booklet pages. There is an excellent explanation of the three main specialisms of ocean, marine and shore-based engineering, plus all you need to know on courses and qualifications. If you are looking for work, check out the recruitment pages for jobs and make use of the journals that may help you to keep in the know and to be better prepared at interview.

★★★ (CLCI: RAV)

Institute of Petroleum **petroleum.co.uk**

Shame there is no five-star category, as this site would surely qualify. Your best bet is to go straight to the 'drop down menu' and careers to more easily identify the wealth of careers and education information available. You will immediately find encouraging details promoting lifelong learning and training opportunities. There is masses of advice for students and a host of informative links for those seeking recruitment or researching the industry.

★★★ (CLCI: ROB)

Institution of Chemical Engineers **icheme.org**

This site has all the right ingredients to help you plan a future in chemical engineering. The excellent careers pages within whynotchemeng have everything from asking basic questions about the profession to case studies of individuals and course titles with links to appropriate universities. Employment opportunities will link you to potential companies, but go back to the main site and Situations vacant for IChemE's own recruitment information. Also, don't miss the training and CPD pages, a new on-line book catalogue, which was under development at the time of writing and a number of journals and magazine articles tucked away within information.

★★★ (CLCI: RAG)

Jewellery **ganoksin.com/borisat/nenam/career.htm**

It may be in the USA, it may be a long web address, but the careers information on a wide range of jewellery-related specialisms is just excellent.

★ (CLCI: ROZ)

Motor Industry Training Council **mitc.co.uk**

This is more the official site for the industry, but once you have checked it through pop into the motor careers section, which has some excellent sources of help and advice. For example, different job roles are described, there are informative pages on training and qualifications as well as an interactive quiz. The parent site is noteworthy for its regional information in Scotland, Wales and Northern Ireland.

★★   (CLCI: RAE)

National Electrotechnical Training   **net-works.org.uk**

Good site for training information and links with schools and colleges. Career pages are limited, but complemented well by 'a range of useful case studies' for more detail.

★★   (CLCI: RAK)

Paper Federation of Great Britain   **paper.org.uk**

Head for careers and the 'careers in the paper industry' pages but you will eventually be drawn into other sites and more detailed information. There is useful content on opportunities age 16 and 18, as well as scholarships and bursaries, but don't miss the career paths section, which clearly shows just how far you could go in the industry.

★   (CLCI: SAP)

Powergen   **pgen.com**

Students and graduates interested in a range of technical, scientific and commercial careers will benefit from checking out the jobs section on this site. There looks to be useful undergraduate placement opportunities and the case studies are both extensive and very informative. Powergen is increasing its business overseas and looking to expand, and so is well worth keeping in touch with if you have other skills, particularly linguistic, to offer.

★★   (CLCI: RAN)

Royal Aeronautical Society   **raes.org.uk**

A good site if you want to find out about the aeronautical industry, as well as courses in higher education that are accredited by the RAS. Vacancy and placement information is being added, and hopefully careers information in the future.

★   (CLCI: RAC)

Royal Institute of Naval Architecture   rina.org.uk

You can access the full text of a booklet *Careers in Naval Architecture* at this site, which includes information on courses and qualifications. There are also some useful details on continuing professional development for those already established in the profession, and good international links to organisations employing naval architects. If looking towards scholarships and awards, check out the institution pages.

★★   (CLCI: ROF)

Steel UK   steel.org.uk

Facts and figures seem to pour out of this site and are probably useful for supporting project work in schools and colleges. Also of interest, particularly to teachers, will be the schools resources pages that cover from primary to sixth form. The careers and training profiles are brief but good, covering a broad range of jobs in the industry, but for more detailed information you really must drop into the Steel and Metals NTO and particularly the recruitment and careers pages at **sinto.co.uk**.

★   (CLCI: SAM)

Telecommunications & Call Centres   e-skills.com

E-Skills are now responsible for addressing the IT and Telecoms skills needs of employers in the UK. They also oversee two different business sectors including Call2Change for the Call/Contact Centre sector, and IT4all for IT user skills.

UK Steel Association   uksteel.org.uk

The careers pages are excellent, particularly if you want to see where your education can lead and the ratio of jobs to types of qualifications (see where the jobs are). Don't miss scrolling down to the address pages which suggest organisations you can approach for work across the UK. This site is worthy of wider research using the site map and link pages.

★★★   (CLCI: SAM)

Welding Institute	twi.co.uk

This site gets few points for ease of navigation, but if you're already a skilled welder, then there is plenty here to complement your welding experience to date, as well as take you into new skill areas. Check out the job knowledge and technology file pages within the site map. If looking for a change of scene, look to the job vacancies section. But for careers information you need to put careers into the search box and then you will find some really useful information.

★★   (CLCI: RON)

Other Sites of Interest

Agricultural Engineering	silsoe.cranfield.ac.uk
Aircraft Maintenance	flsaerospace.com
Ames Consultancy	ames.co.uk
Association of the British Pharmaceutical Association	abpi.org.uk
Association of Mining Analysts	ama.org.uk
Baker	bakers.co.uk
Biscuits, Cake, Chocolate and Confectionery Alliance	bccca.org.uk
BP Futures	bpfutures.com
BreWorld (brewing industry)	breworld.com
British Artists Blacksmiths Association	baba.org.uk
British Energy	british-energy.com
British Furniture Manufacturers	bfm.org.uk
British Gas	gas.co.uk
British Horological Institute	bhi.co.uk
British Marine Industries Federation	bmif.co.uk
British National Space Centre	bnsc.gov.uk
British Nuclear Fuels	bnfl.com
British Polymer Training Association	bpta.co.uk
British Printing Industries Federation	bpif.org.uk
British Telecom	bt.com
Cable & Wireless College	cwcollege.com
Cadbury's	cadbury.co.uk
Chartered Institute of Building Services Engineers	cibse.org
Chemical Industries Association	cia.org.uk
Chemical Manufacturing	sourcerer.co.uk
Communications Management Association	thecma.com
Cranfield College of Aeronautics	cranfield.ac.uk/coa
Dairy Training and Development Council	milk.co.uk

Electrical Training Opportunities	**jtlimited.co.uk**
Electricity Association	**electricity.org.uk**
Electricity Training Association	**eta.org.uk**
Engineer – British Airways	**baengineer.co.uk**
Engineering Construction Industry Training Board	**ecitb.org.uk**
Engineering Council	**engc.org.uk**
Engineering Manufacturing	**emta.org.uk**
Engineering Recruitment Shows	**engrecruitshow.co.uk**
Engineering Services Training Trust	**estt.org.uk**
Engineering Training Council – Northern Ireland	**etcni.org.uk**
Engineering World Forum	**eng-tips.com**
Enginuity!	**enginuity.org.uk**
Executive Recruitment Services	**ers.co.uk**
Federation of Communcation Services	**fcs.org.uk**
Fibre-optic Industry Association	**fibreoptic.org.uk**
Ford Motor Company	**ford.co.uk**
Gas Industry National Training Organisation	**ginto.co.uk**
Glass Training Ltd	**glass-training.co.uk**
Healthcare Products, Coatings and Chemicals	**akzonobel.com**
Heating, Ventilating, Air-Conditioning and Refrigeration	**esttl.org.uk**
IBM	**ibm.com**
Institute of Acoustics	**ioa.org.uk**
Institute of Domestic Heating and Environmental Engineers	**idhe.org.uk**
Institute of Energy	**instenergy.org.uk**
Institute of Highway Incorporated Engineers	**ihie.org.uk**
Institute of Mining and Metallurgy	**imm.org.uk**
Institute of Packaging	**iop.co.uk**
Institute of Paper	**instpaper.org.uk**
Institute of Physics and Engineering in Medicine	**ipem.org.uk**
Institute of Printing	**globalprint.com./uk/iop**
Institution of Agricultural Engineers	**iagre.org**
Institution of Electrical Engineers	**iee.org.uk**
Institution of Engineering Designers	**ied.org.uk**
Institution of Gas Engineers	**igaseng.com**
Institution of Incorporated Engineers	**iie.org.uk**
Intel	**intel.com**
JIB for Electrical Contracting Industry	**jib.org.uk**
Man-made Fibres Industry Training Organisation	**man-made-fibres.co.uk**
Marconi Recruitment	**msi-world.com**
Matchtech Engineering (Technical Recruitment Consultancy)	**matchtech.co.uk**

Meat Training Council	**meattraining.org.uk**
Mechanical Engineering	**imeche.org.uk**
Mineral Industries Educational Trust	**miet.org.uk**
Motor Careers	**motor-careers.co.uk**
Motorola Careers	**motorolacareers.com**
NASA Jobs	**nasajobs.nasa.gov**
National Association of Goldsmiths	**progold.net**
National Association of Paper Merchants	**napm.org.uk**
Nokia Careers	**nokia.co.uk/careers**
Oil Gas Extraction	**opito.com**
Paper Education and Training Council	**papertrain.net**
Pianoforte Tuners' Association	**pianotuner.org.uk**
Powertechnology	**powertech.co.uk**
Print Wizard	**printwizard.co.uk**
Pulp, Paper and Board Industry	**ppic.org.uk**
Recruitment Holdings Ltd	**rhl.co.uk**
Royal Airforce College Cranwell	**cranwell.raf.mod.uk**
Recruitment IEE	**iee.org.uk**
Shell	**shell.com**
Specialists in Engineering and Technical Recruitment	**recruitmentregister.com**
The Smallpiece Trust	**smallpiece.co.uk**
Society of British Aerospace Companies	**sbac.co.uk**
Sound and Audio Engineering College	**sae.edu**
Steel and Metals Industry	**sinto.co.uk**
Technical Recruitment Specialists	**jprecruit.com**
Telecommunications	**ntotele.com**
Telecommunications Industry Association	**tia.org.uk**
UK Offshore Operators Association	**oilandgas.org.uk**
Underwater Centre	**stenmar.com**
United Kingdom Atomic Energy Authority	**ukaea.org.uk**
Women in Science, Engineering and Technology	**set4women.gov.uk**

CONSTRUCTION AND LAND SERVICES
CLCI CODES: U–UZ

Organisations and Work Environment
Offices, building sites and portakabins, workshops, shopping centres, hospitals, schools, factories, private homes and clubs, farms, garden centres, educational institutions, public parks and gardens, heritage sites, leisure centres, theme parks, forests and woodlands, research centres, conservation and country parks.

The Jobs

Surveyor	Building Services Engineer	Glazier
Archaeological Surveyor	Bricklayer	Felt Roofer
Agricultural Surveyor	Joiner	Carpenter
Mining/Mineral Surveyor	Construction Manager	Scaffolder
Quantity Surveyor	Builder's Labourer	Builder
Architect	Painter and Decorator	Ceiling Fixer
Architectural Technician	Structural Engineer	Mason
Landscape Architect	Road Maintenance	Fencer
Auctioneer	Construction Technician	Estimator
Valuer	Civil Engineer	Clerk of Works
Rent Officer	Plant Operator	Pipe Fitter
Public Health Engineer	Building Conservation	Crane Operator
Cartographer	Water Engineer	Site Engineer
Ordnance Survey	Drainage Engineer	Housing Manager

If you are having difficulty locating a suitable building contractor, visit the Chartered Building Company's site at **ciob.org.uk**. The careers pages are brief, but useful. Again, if it is a registered plumber you need, then **plumbers.org.uk** has all the details. This is the site for the Institute of Plumbing and is well worth a visit; also if you are already trained but looking for further professional development. Alternatively, if you are job-hunting or just wanting a change of scene, you will find the Directory of Industrial Associates an excellent resource for contacts. Still related to construction, but more concerned with social housing issues, is the Housing Corporation which you can find at **housingcorp.gov.uk**. There is also information for home-seekers and tenants, but do also check out the links to other sites which will give you some excellent sources for further research. It may not be common knowledge that virtual reality is one of the newest technologies used by landscape architects, but for further gems on courses at colleges and universities as well as careers help do drop into **l-i.org.uk**.

British Institute of Architectural Technologists · **biat.org.uk**

Aspiring architectural technologists will enjoy this site which has all the essential careers information. There is a good introduction to the type of work and qualities required for this specialist profession. Details are tucked within the education pages and include good listings and access to appropriate universities, an NVQ centre and useful links. Relevant courses will be of interest to some international students, as they list qualifications recognised by the Institute for

associate membership.
★★ (CLCI: UB)

British Plumbing Employers Council · bpec.org.uk

The careers information on plumbing is particularly good at this site, as it asks key questions such as: What is it like to be a professional plumber, what skills or qualifications do I need and are there very many career opportunities? Employers looking to employ young people on Modern Apprenticeships or National Traineeship can also pick up useful advice and valuable information on NVQ/SVQ qualifications.
★★ (CLCI: UF)

Chartered Institute of Housing · cih.org

It is so encouraging to come across a site which clearly makes every effort to encourage first career, graduates and job changes into this fast developing and topical industry. It is recommended that you research the careers in housing and working in housing sections together, as the latter includes useful qualification and training information. Graduate entry is well covered, and distance learning is a useful option explored further in services. The personal comments from those already in the profession may be hand-picked, but are still very helpful. Social Science students researching housing issues will benefit from dropping into housing agenda and related sites.
★★ (CLCI: UH)

Construction Industrial Training Board · citb.org.uk

This site is just excellent and will be a huge help to anyone interested in a career in the construction industry. The careers options pages are packed with key questions you might wish to ask, as well as great insights into some of the trades and specialisms from people actually doing the jobs (see Nine Lives). There are learning resource pages for schools and a very good A–Z guide to qualifications which relate to all the careers you can specialise in.
★★ (CLCI: UF)

Engineering Construction Industry Training Board · ecitb.org.uk

One of the many excellent features of this site, which includes training and qualifications in engineering construction, is the careers pages. You have the opportunity to explore craft, technician and professional careers, with case study and personal profile material.

★★ (CLCI: UN)

Institution of Civil Engineers ice.org.uk

Don't be confused, but you need to go to the student pages, rather than careers, for all the occupational information. There is masses of useful information on civil engineering, courses and qualifications at university as well as opportunities for continuing professional development. If you wish to get sponsorship, scholarships or even work experience advice, then check out the learning curve zone. There is also plenty of help in the Jobs pages with links to a specialist recruitment agency.

★★★ (CLCI: UN)

National Association of Estate Agency naea.co.uk

The general public section includes careers and training information as well as other topical areas that either influence or form an integral part of the industry.

★★ (CLCI: UM)

Royal Institute of British Architects architecture.com

Head straight for the careers section and you are greeted with a highly impressive topic menu, which would appeal as much to urban and environmental research students as to aspiring architects! For the vocationally minded there are very useful career profiles complemented nicely by life as a student stories. There is even brief, but helpful details on financing oneself through the 5-year degree course. For year-out or full employment there is always RIBA's own on-line vacancy help at **riba-jobs.com**.

★★★ (CLCI: UB)

Royal Institution of Chartered Surveyors rics.org.uk/careers

This site seems to have it all, whether you are aspiring to be a surveyor, looking for a career change or needing help after being made redundant. The how to qualify pages are an ideal place to start if looking to gain an RICS chartered surveying qualification. The university link's

search facility will identify courses both in the UK and overseas with an opportunity to visit appropriate sites for further information. For careers information, check out the What is surveying pages which include a useful introduction to at least nine different surveying specialisms. The jobs section taking you to **jobsin.co.uk/surveying** helps you seek work, as well as enables you to post your CV on-line. There is even an imaginative option to undergo a psychometric profile, currently costing £15 to help clarify and confirm current aspirations.

★★★   (CLCI: UM)

Other Sites of Interest

1st Landscape	**1stlandscape.co.uk**
Architecture	**designforhomes.org**
Architectural Association	**archinet.co.uk**
Architecture and Surveying Institute	**asi.org.uk**
British Cartographic Society	**cartography.org.uk**
British Wood Preserving and Damp Proofing Association	**bwpda.co.uk**
Building Services Engineering	**cibse.org**
Chartered Institute of Building Services	**ciob.org.uk**
Chartered Institute of Housing	**cih.org**
Chartered Institute of Water and Environmental Management	**ciwem.org.uk**
College of Estate Management	**cem.ac.uk**
Construction Industry Discussion Forum (CITB)	**bconstructive.co.uk**
Construction Industry Training Board for Northern Ireland	**citbni.org.uk**
Contract Flooring Association	**cfa.org.uk**
Engineering Council	**engc.org.uk**
Heating Ventilating Contractors Association	**hvca.org.uk**
Housing Corporation	**housingcorp.gov.uk**
Housing Potential	**key-potential.co.uk**
Institute of Ecology & Environmental Management	**ieem.org.uk**
Institute of Plumbing	**plumbers.org.uk**
Institute of Revenues, Rating and Valuation	**irv.org.uk**
Institution of Civil Engineering Surveyors	**ices.org.uk**
International Civil Engineering Projects (USA)	**hatch.com**
Landscape Architecture	**keengroup.demon.co.uk**
Landscape Design Trust	**landscape.co.uk**
Landscape Institute	**l-i.org.uk**
MacDonald Surveyors Recruiting Services	**macdonald.co.uk**
National Association of Estate Agents	**naea.co.uk**
National Housing Federation	**housing.org.uk**

Ordnance Survey	**ordsvy.gov.uk**
Planning Magazine Online	**planning.haynet.com**
Property Information	**propertyatfreeman.com**
Property Services	**psnto.org**
Royal Incorporation of Architects in Scotland	**rias.org.uk**
Royal Town Planning Institute	**rtpi.org.uk**
Smarter Builder Training	**smarter-builder.co.uk**
Thomas Telford Training	**t-telford.co.uk**

LAND USE
CLCI CODES: W–WAZ

The Jobs

Woodland Manager	Farmer	Dairy Farmer
Tree Surgeon	Poultry Worker	Beekeeper
Forester	Farm Secretary	Pig Farmer
Forest/Park Warden	Herdsman/Woman	Fruit Grower
Market Gardener	Shepherd/Shepherdess	Stockman
Game Warden	Nature Conservationist	Nursery Worker
Garden Centre Assistant	Garden Centre Manager	

Not designed for the casual visitor, but with much current interest in looking after our land resources, the British Crop Protection Council at **bcpc.org** has some very useful information. The Corporate Members pages (within About Us) are very good for locating other organisations which have a direct interest and influence in this area. Farmers are also much in the news at the moment with a great deal of concern about their traditional livelihood being undermined by political, health and enviromental issues, sadly influenced by events well beyond their acreage. The National Farmers Union site at **nfu.org.uk** will certainly keep you informed on the issues, but is also a brilliant resource for representing the industry in many other practical ways. Perhaps your interests lean more specifically towards conservation, but spiced with exploration and adventure. These voluntary-based projects are certainly not for the faint-hearted, as they normally run in tropical countries. However, it could be a great way to launch your career in habitat and wildlife conservation; if you are still keen, check out **frontierprojects.ac.uk**.

Countryside Agency   countryside.gov.uk

An impressive site by any standards, with masses of information on the environment, transportation and conservation. Visit the reception area for current job information and our work to get a real feel for the issues in the rural economy.

★   (CLCI: SAW)

Department of Environment, Food and Rural Affairs   defra.gov.uk

This has everything from Foot and Mouth, BSE and quarantine regulations to international trade and animal welfare as well as a great deal of information on food and land-based industries. Brilliant for project work, but there is little on careers except within the recruitment section.

★   (CLCI: W/WAL)

Environmental Information for Industry   ifi.co.uk

This site scores particularly on its joblink service, which lists an impressive number of vocational and business-related vacancies in environmental work. There is also a useful reference to recruitment agencies, an opportunity to read extracts from a number of specialist environmental journals and an excellent training course calendar.

★   (CLCI: WAR)

Greenpeace International   greenpeace.org

This site has to be rated, just for the sheer volume of amazing data. Every kind of topical as well as lesser-known environmental issues are explored. You can also use their extensive web links to locate further gems. The political arm can be located at **gn.apc.org**.

★   (CLCI: WAR)

Institute of Horticulture   horticulture.org.uk

Impressive front pages lead you to a wealth of information about the horticultural industry. The education in horticulture section is a useful port of call as its course advice pages are excellent for young school leavers and undergraduates, as well as mature applicants looking to gain suitable qualifications for the industry. Don't miss the link pages if you want to check out unusual items like alpine gardening or information on the professional journal.

★★ (CLCI: WAD)

Land Based Industries   lantra.co.uk

Brilliant! There is not enough space to comment on how informative, helpful and inspiring the careers information, personal case study details, and education and training pages are on this site. The labour market information is impressive and confirms just how crucial Lantra is in representing 1.5 million people and 360,000 businesses in the land-based industries. Late entrants may benefit from going to the site map and agenda training pages for information on open courses. It was only the lack of job-hunting advice that stopped this site getting the three-star rating!

★★ (CLCI: U)

Royal Horticultural Society   rhs.org.uk

If you have an interest in horticulture, then you will enjoy this well-presented and informative site. There is very good information on RHS courses within the education and examinations parts of the site, as well as a helpful list of accredited colleges throughout the UK and Ireland.

★ (CLCI: WAD)

Other Sites of Interest

ADAS (international consultancy to land-based industries)	adas.co.uk
Agriculture Online (USA)	agriculture.com
Association of Professional Foresters	apfs.demon.co.uk
Biotechnology and Biological Sciences Research Council	bbsrc.ac.uk
British Association for Shooting and Conservation	basc.org.uk
British Crop Protection Council	bcpc.org
British International Golf Greenkeepers Association	bigga.co.uk
Chartered Institute of Water and Environmental Management	ciwem.org.uk
Countryside Council for Wales	ccw.gov.uk
Dairy Training and Development Council	dairytraining.org.uk
Dept of Agriculture & Rural Development for NI	dani.gov.uk
Environment Agency	environment-agency.gov.uk
Environment Agency Wales	environment-agency.wales.gov.uk
Environmental Data Services	ends.co.uk
Farming and Countryside Education	face-online.org.uk

Farming Online	**farmline.com**
Forest Service for Northern Ireland	**dani.gov.uk/forestry**
Forestry Commission of Great Britain	**forestry.gov.uk**
Forestry Land Use Internet Resources	**forestry.bangor.ac.uk**
Forestry Service of Northern Ireland	**dani.gov.uk/forestry**
Friends of the Earth	**foe.co.uk**
Frontier-Conservation through Exploration	**frontierprojects.ac.uk**
Game Conservancy Trust	**game-conservancy.org.uk**
Garden Links	**gardenlinks.ndo.co.uk**
The Green Channel	**greenchannel.com**
Green Net	**gn.apc.org**
Growing Careers	**growing-careers.com**
Institute of Arable Crops Research	**iacr.bbsrc.ac.uk**
International Plant Index	**ipni.org**
International Plant Information	**http://life.csu.edu.au/iopi**
Land Based Industries	**lantra.co.uk**
National Council for the Conservation of Plants and Gardens	**nccpg.org.uk**
National Farmers Union	**nfu.org.uk**
National Park Service (USA)	**nps.gov**
National Playing Fields Association	**npfa.co.uk**
The National Trust	**nationaltrust.org.uk**
National Trust for Scotland	**nts.org.uk**
Natural History Museum	**nhm.ac.uk**
Nature	**nature.com**
Oxford Forestry Institute	**plants.ox.ac.uk/ofi**
Royal Agricultural Society	**rase.org.uk**
Royal Botanic Garden Edinburgh	**rbge.org.uk**
Royal Botanic Gardens	**rbgkew.org.uk**
Rural Business Network	**rbnet.co.uk**
Scottish Executive Rural Affairs Dept	**scotland.gov.uk/who/dept_rural.asp**
Soil Association	**soilassociation.org**
UK Turf Industry	**turfpages.com**

Part Two

Education
and
Training

7
Education
and Training

The previous chapters can and do provide much encouragement and valuable advice for your careers research. However, at this stage it may be more important that you secure the next appropriate step in your education, rather than worry about any long-term career plans. While the ultimate goal may be a career that is fulfilling and prosperous, it is perfectly acceptable to delay such decisions and concentrate on more immediate concerns; for example, what course am I likely to enjoy, for what period of study, and will it encourage me to reach my full potential and keep my options open for the future? Of equal value is the individual who plans a very specific, sometimes vocational orientated course with a particular career in mind.

It is possible to access an excellent range of education and training directories in most of the larger careers offices up and down the country. There is often valuable advice to help your research of appropriate resources and other agencies. Most offices and the larger public libraries provide free Internet access, and then there are cyber cafés and the like. What is exciting is that the world wide web provides an alternative and constantly updating medium on educational information and opportunities to suit almost any individual's needs. Lifelong learning is now at the centre of government policy with every encouragement given to develop existing skills and knowledge as well as start new ventures in education. The development of Learn Direct and UKOnline centres up and down the country are providing just such opportunities for adults. The information and technological age is looking to be complemented by the oncoming learning era with a tremendous growth in on-line learning and training direct into your home or workplace.

This chapter includes sites that link to educational institutions and professional bodies, as well as all the main national training organisations. It is designed as much for young people and students, as for teachers looking for educational resources on the Internet and to inspire those not currently involved in education. There are details of courses in general, further and higher education, and advice on finance, qualifications, studying abroad, gap year opportunities and application to university.

CHOOSING COURSES AND QUALIFICATIONS
CLCI CODES: AT–ATB

General Education Schools and Sixth Form Colleges
Despite the bold claims made by many sites, few if any provide a totally comprehensive search facility. However, **schoolzone.co.uk** is one of the better ones, particularly for junior and secondary level searching. There is also **schoolsearch.co.uk** for Independent Schools complemented by the very informative Independent Schools Council Information Service at **isis.org.uk**. If boarding schools are an important consideration, visit the Hobsons Guide to UK Boarding Schools at **boardingschools.hobsons.com**. There is just so much to explore off the Internet, but don't miss the highly acclaimed **kevinsplayroom.co.uk** for GCSE subject information and study help. Also, **schoolnet.co.uk** for foundation, keystages 1–4 and post-16 information.

The Sites
Basic Skills Agency	**basic-skills.co.uk**
Department for Education and Skills (DfES)	**dfes.gov.uk**
Department of Education for Northern Ireland	**deni.gov.uk**
Education Links (USA)	**educationindex.com**
Education Resources on the Internet	**topmarks.co.uk**
Girls' Schools Association	**girls-schools.org.uk**
Hobsons Guide to UK Boarding Schools	**boardingschools.hobsons.com**
Independent Schools Council Information Service	**isis.org.uk**
National Bureau for Students with Disabilities	**skill.org.uk**
The National Curriculum	**nc.uk.net**
National Curriculum Subject Links	**kevinsplayroom.co.uk**
Primary Education	**einsteinonline.co.uk**
School Search	**schoolsearch.co.uk**
Which Way Now Subject Options	**dfes.gov.uk/whichwaynow**

Further and Higher Education
Two sites well worth checking out before going on to college or university are **hotcourses.com** and **dfes.gov.uk/iyc**. The front-runner in providing a quick link to further and higher education must be the University of Wolverhampton at **scit.wlv.ac.uk**, as its Active Maps takes you from a national or regional map directly to the institution's own web site. However, it is worth checking others listed, particularly if you wish to broaden your search to include specific courses of interest. Choosing a further education course or deciding the right place to spend the next

three or four years of your life at university is not always easy. However, by using **opendays.com**, visiting institutions and talking to teaching staff, your chances of making the right choice improves significantly. If you live outside the UK, Hobsons at **studyuk.hobson.com** is brilliant and will tell you all you need to know, including accommodation, costs, travel and adapting to life in the UK. **ucas.com** is essential viewing and one to keep coming back to if you are thinking about or actively planning to launch into higher education. This site also includes excellent information for mature students within the advice pages.

The Sites

Association of Commonwealth Universities	**acu.ac.uk**
UniversitiesUK	**universitiesuk.ac.uk**
Conference for Independent Further Education	**cife.org.uk**
Further Education Funding Council	**fefc.ac.uk**
Higher Education Institutions	**niss.ac.uk**
Higher Education Subject Information	**bubl.ac.uk**
Higher Education Staff Development Agency	**hesda.org.uk**
Hot Courses	**hotcourses.com**
Independent Schools Careers Organisation	**isco.org.uk**
Independent Schools Search	**schoolsearch.co.uk**
Janet UK Academic and Research Network	**ja.net**
Learning and Skills Development Agency	**feda.ac.uk**
Links to Further and Higher Education Institutions	**scit.wlv.ac.uk**
National Bureau for Students with Disabilities	**skill.org.uk**
New Dept for Employment and Learning – Northern Ireland	**delni.gov.uk**
Open University	**open.ac.uk**
Postgraduate Course Information	**postgrad.hobsons.com**
Postgraduat.Com	**postgraduat.com**
PUSH Online (Which University)	**push.co.uk**
Springboard Student Services	**springboard.hobsons.com**
Trait Education – HE Search	**thecoursesource.co.uk**
UCAS HE course listing, etc.	**ucas.com**
UK Course Discover-software	**ecctis.co.uk**
University & College Research Organisation	**hero.ac.uk**
University Association for Contemporary European Studies	**uaces.org**
Worldwide MBAs	**editionxii.co.uk**

Qualifications and Standards

You cannot make a better start than the Qualifications and Curriculum Authority at **qca.org.uk** if you want to know about anything from National Curriculum subjects at junior school and secondary level to higher and further education and academic, as well as vocational qualifications. Standards in education is a topical issue, so it is little surprise that the government hosts such a site at **standards.dfes.gov.uk** which is designed to provide guidance and the tools to help schools improve effectiveness, raise standards and reduce workload.

The Sites

Associated Examing Board / SEG	**aeb.org.uk**
Assessment and Qualifications Alliance	**aqa.org.uk**
A / AS-Levels	**alevels.com**
AS-Levels	**bbc.co.uk/education/asguru**
British Accreditation Council for Independent Further and Higher Education	**the-bac.org**
BTEC / Edexcel	**edexcel.org.uk**
City and Guilds	**city-and-guilds.co.uk**
Foundation Degree	**foundationdegree.org.uk**
GCSEs	**gcse.com**
GCSE, GNVQ and A-Levels	**dfes.gov.uk/qualifications**
International Baccalaureate	**ibo.org**
National Curriculum Online	**nc.uk.net**
National Vocational Qualifications	**dfes.gov.uk/nvq**
Northern Examinations and Assessment Board	**neab.ac.uk**
Northern Ireland Council for Curriculum Examination and Assessment	**ccea.org.uk**
OFSTED	**ofsted.gov.uk**
Oxford, Cambridge and RSA Examinations	**ocr.org.uk**
Qualifications, Curriculum and Assessment Authority for Wales	**accac.org.uk**
Qualifications and Curriculum Authority	**qca.org.uk**
Scottish Qualifications Authority	**sqa.org.uk**
Standards in Education (DfES)	**standards.dfes.gov.uk**
Welsh Joint Education Committee	**wjec.co.uk**

Lifelong Learning

There has never been a better time for encouraging returners to education. While it can be a leisure interest, there is always the possibility of developing further knowledge and skills that can boost your present career, or give you the confidence to have another crack at those dormant aspirations and dreams. If you feel that your earlier education experience is holding you back, rather than encouraging the untapped potential within, then be encouraged at **basic-skills.co.uk**. You can then explore your situation nearer home, as most local schools, colleges and adult education centres offer a range of basic skills courses and have done so for many years. You may have noticed that Learn Direct centres are springing up all over the country, so to find out your nearest centre visit **learndirect.co.uk**. It could well be that these first tentative steps later open up the Access route into higher education, so **ucas.com/access** may appeal. Perhaps the first desire is to become more IT literate and again massive opportunities beckon and then, if you want, to study for almost any qualification from your own home. If a weekend taster is more what you're looking for, then check out your nearest adult residential college at **aredu.org.uk**. You really are spoilt for choice, but just to tease out further potential, why not visit the BBC's renowned Education Learning Zone at **bbc.co.uk/education/lzone** or the UK Lifelong Learning web site at **lifelonglearning.co.uk** which includes examples of individuals who have made use of Career Development Loans to pursue their interests.

The Sites

Access Routes into Higher Education	**ucas.com/access**
Association of British Correspondence Courses	**homestudy.org.uk**
BBC Education Learning Zone	**bbc.co.uk/education/lzone**
British Association of Open Learnng	**baol.co.uk**
Foundation Degree	**foundationdegree.org.uk**
Learn Direct	**learndirect.co.uk**
National Extension College	**nec.ac.uk**
National Grid for Learning	**ngfl.gov.uk**
National Institute for Adult Continuing Education	**niace.org.uk**
Open and Distance Learning Quality Council	**odlqc.org.uk**
Open College of the Arts	**oca-uk.com**
Open Learning Centre International	**olc.ccta.ac.uk**
Open University	**open.ac.uk**
Open University Online Catalogue	**ouw.co.uk**
Time off for Study and Training	**dfes.gov.uk/tfst**
UK and Worldwide Distance Learning Directories	**distance-learning.co.uk**
UK Lifelong Learning	**lifelonglearning.co.uk**
Univesity for Industry	**ufiltd.co.uk**
University of the Third Age – Lifelong Learning	**u3a.org.uk**
Workers' Educational Association	**wea.org.uk**

Studying Abroad

There is no better place to explore worldwide education systems that off the hugely helpful European Council for International Schools site at

ecis.org. More and more older students are exploring the possiblity of continuing their studies abroad. If looking to the continent then Careers Europe at **careerseurope.co.uk** is a good place to start. There is also a rich source to tap into from the Association of Commonwealth Universities at **acu.ac.uk**. However, if the USA is part of your plans, then you simply must check out The Fulbright Commission at **fulbright.co.uk**. They can provide all the information you need, including the essential SAT preparation for university applications, as well as the latest news on postgraduate awards. In fact, if you are looking to study in almost any other country you will find a great companion at another US site, **studyabroad.com**.

The Sites

Association of Commonwealth Universities	**acu.ac.uk**
British Council	**britcoun.org**
Canadian Universities	**aucc.ca**
Careers Europe	**careerseurope.co.uk**
Central Applications Office Ireland	**cao.ie**
Council on International Educational Exchange	**ciee.org**
European Council of International Schools	**ecis.org**
The Fulbright Commission	**fulbright.co.uk**
International Student Exchange	**aiesec.org**
Studying Abroad (USA)	**studyabroad.com**
Learning Opportunities UK and Australia	**studylink.com**

APPLICATIONS TO UNIVERSITIES AND SPECIALIST COLLEGES
CLCI CODE: ATC

There is room for more web sites on applying to courses in general, but the BBC is at hand with hugely helpful advice whether age 16+ leaving school or 18+ looking at careers or university. Check out **bbc.co.uk/radio1/essentials/student**. University and Colleges Admissions Service (UCAS) has an excellent site at **studentuk.com** which also covers a host of other issues related to student life. You will also find links to their main site at **ucas.com**. Parents often feel out in the cold at such times, so will no doubt welcome the pages encouraging their support. The online application procedure is getting off to rather a shaky start, but is a good one to keep in touch with. The hunt is always on for more teachers, but what subjects are the current flavour and how to apply? Check out the Graduate Teacher Training Registry at **gttr.ac.uk**. For applicants to training for other professions, such as nursing, social work, etc., do visit appropriate career sections in other parts of this publication.

The Sites

Graduate Teacher Training Registry	**gttr.ac.uk**
Student Essentials	**bbc.co.uk/radio1/essentials/student**
UCAS (Universities and Colleges Admissions Service)	**ucas.com**
UCAS – Student Site	**studentuk.com**

FINANCE AND RECORDS OF ACHIEVEMENT
CLCI CODES: ATD–ATE

The Internet is a great tool for accessing information that is normally very difficult to track down. Finance is a good example, as is the Student Union itself at **nusonline.co.uk**. Information on student loans can be found at the Student Loan Company site at **slc.co.uk** – a non-departmental government organisation tasked with administering publicly financed loans for students. Also, **namss.org.uk** is well worth a visit. Should unsecured debts creep in, then an excellent site worth its weight in gold is **debtloans.co.uk** for help and advice. If you are disabled, you cannot do better than visit the National Bureau for Students with Disabilities at **skill.org.uk** who can draw on masses of experience to help you. There are also potential charities and trusts that you can contact through **funderfinder.org.uk**. If you have a desire to compete for scholarship places then try **scholarshipsearch.org.uk**. For sponsorship details visit your nearest local or main careers centre as they are likely to have a number of useful reference books. Also check out your career interests in the relevant chapters of this book.

Employers of the future will be heartened by the fact that over 87% of recent school-leavers have National Records of Achievement to their name. To find out more on this initiative to recognise, record and evaluate achievements, check out **dfes.gov.uk/nra**.

The Sites

Awards for Arts Humanities	**ahrb.ac.uk**
European Funding	**efc.be**
Financial Support in Higher Education	**dfee.gov.uk/studentsupport**
Funder Finder	**funderfinder.org.uk**
The Further Education Funding Council	**fefc.ac.uk**
Higher Education Funding Council for England	**hefce.ac.uk**
National Bureau for Students with Disabilities	**skill.org.uk**
National Postgraduate Commiteee	**npc.org.uk**
National Record of Achievement	**dfes.gov.uk/nra**

National Union of Students	**nusonline.co.uk**
Northern Ireland Student Movement	**nistudents.com**
Personal Finance Education Group	**pfeg.org.uk**
Postgraduate Scholarship Information	**postgrad.hobsons.com**
Scholarship Search	**scholarship-search.org.uk**
Scottish Higher Education Funding Council	**shefc.ac.uk**
Student Advice	**hobsons.com**
Student Awards Agency for Scotland	**student-support-saas.gov.uk**
Student Loans Company	**slc.co.uk**
UK Reseach Councils	**research-councils.ac.uk**
Welsh Funding Council	**wfc.ac.uk**

STUDENT LIFE AND GAP YEAR
CLCI CODE: ATF

Why not save yourself hours of heartache and prepare for life at university by checking out a number of useful sites first? The National Union of Students site at **nusonline.co.uk** is a great place to start, as they specialise in most student life and welfare matters. Also **push.co.uk** has great hints and tips on a wide range of highly relevant issues, as does **namss.org.uk**, including adult and continuing education. UK and overseas students are offered a rich feast of helpful advice at **hobsons.com**. This is the age of the young international traveller. Never has there been such a wealth of opportunities to attract school pupils, students and graduates alike to seek adventure and pastures global. Many employers look very favourably on applicants who have gained such experiences. It seems many older folk are also taking to the skies, and in many cases offering their considerable life experience to needy parts of the world. An excellent portal site to start your research is **yearoutgroup.org** who at the time of writing had 22 organisations you could hot-boot into! STA travel at **statravel.co.uk** provides helpful advice to students as well as the independent traveller, as does **peridot.co.uk/gapyear**. Another to look out for is **worldwidevolunteering.org.uk** which offers a taster to their amazing directory listing 800 organisations and over 250,000 placements in the UK and overseas. Those whose passion is sailing will love **sunsail.com** or the Sail Training Association which offers 'the experience of a lifetime' for young people, adults, the unemployed and the disabled. If you like the idea of big ship sailing why not check them out at **sta.org.uk**. If you're more concerned with world conservation, **frontierprojects.ac.uk** will be of particular interest and perhaps help launch an environmental career. Another site not suited to the faint-hearted is **wse.org.uk** who also operate as a disaster relief agency, but specific skills are likely to be necessary in this instance.

The Sites

Student Exchange, Travel Advice and Accommodation

Academic Year in the USA & Europe	**aaiuk.org**
Crazy Dog Travel Guide	**crazydogtravel.com**
European Work Experience	**cant.ac.uk/exact**
Foreign & Commonwealth Office	**fco.gov.uk**
Funderfinder	**funderfinder.org.uk**
GAP Year Sites & Advice	**peridot.co.uk/gapyear**
Hostel Watch	**hostelwatch.com**
International Exchanges	**councilexchangs.org**
Overseas Student Info	**britcoun.org/eis**
Rough Guides – publishers	**roughguides.com**
Scottish Youth Hostel Association	**syha.org.uk**
Springboard	**springboard.hobsons.com**
STA Travel	**statravel.co.uk**
Travel Health Online	**travelhealth.com**
Vacation Work – publisher	**vacationwork.co.uk**
Youth Hostel Association	**yha.org.uk**

European and International GAP Opportunities

Africa & Asia Venture	**aventure.co.uk**
BUNAC – Working Adventures	**bunac.org**
Gap Activity Projects	**gap.org.uk**
Gap Year	**gapyear.com**
International Voluntary Service	**ivsgbn.demon.co.uk**
Lonely Planet	**lonelyplanet.com**
Project Trust	**projecttrust.org.uk**
Quest Overseas	**quest-overseas.co.uk**
Raleigh International	**raleigh.org.uk**
St David's Africa Trust	**africatrust.gi**
Student Partnership Worldwide	**spw.org**
Toybox – Street Children	**toybox.org**
Trekforce Expeditions	**trekforce.org.uk**
VentureCo-Worldwide	**ventureco-worldwide.com**
World Challenge	**world-challenge.co.uk**
Work Experience USA	**workexperienceusa.com**
Worldwise Directory	**brookes.ac.uk/worldwise**
Yearoutgroup	**yearoutgroup.org**
YHA International	**hostellinginternational.org**

Special Interest and Voluntary Experience

Art History Abroad	**arthistoryabroad.com**
Au Pair America	**aifs.com/aupair**
British Trust for Conservation Volunteers	**btcv.org**
BSES Expeditions	**bses.org.uk**
Camp America Summer Jobs	**campamerica.co.uk**
CESA Languages Abroad	**cesalanguages.com**
Changing Worlds	**changingworlds.co.uk**
Community Service Volunteers	**csv.org.uk**
Duke of Edinburgh's Award	**theaward.org**
Earthwach Institute	**earthwatch.org**
EF International Language Schools	**ef.com**
Encounter – Overland	**encounter-overland.com**
Euro and Key Camps	**eurocamp.com**
Friends of the Earth – Scotland	**foe-scotland.org.uk**
Frontier – Conservation	**frontierprojects.ac.uk**
GAP Year Plus – Watersports	**lmitrainng.com**
Global Vision Internationa	**gvi.co.uk**
i To i International Projects	**i-to-i.com**
InfoYouth GAP Guide	**infoyouth.com**
International Agricultural Exchanges	**agriventure.com**
International Sport	**international-academy.com**
Kibbutz	**kibbutz.org.il**
Leonard Cheshire Volunteers	**lcf.org.uk**
National Centre for Volunteering	**volunteering.org.uk**
PGL Travel	**pgl.co.uk**
Pre-University Course – Venice	**johnhallpre-university.com**
Princes Trust	**princes-trust.org.uk**
Reef & Rainforest Expeditions	**coralcay.org**
Sail Training Association	**sta.org.uk**
Sailing Trust	**cirdan-faramir.co.uk**
Ski & Snow Boarding Canada	**peakleaders.co.uk**
Smallpiece Trust – Engineering	**smallpiecetrust.org.uk**
Teaching & Projects Abroad	**teaching-abroad.co.uk**
Travellers Worldwide	**travellersworldwide.com**
Village Camps Europe	**villagecamps.com**
Voluntary Service Overseas	**vso.org.uk**
Volunteer Development Scotland	**vds.org.uk**
Work Experience (undergraduate)	**ncwe.com**
World Wildlife Fund	**worldwildlife.org**
Worldwide Volunteering (database & publication)	**worldwidevolunteering.org.uk**

Year In Industry	**yini.org.uk**
Year Out Drama	**yearoutdrama.com**
Young Enterprise	**young-enterprise.org.uk**

SKILLS TRAINING

New Learning and Skills Councils pages at **lsc.gov.uk** offer a good insight into arrangements for the funding and planning of education and training for those aged over 16 in England. The LSC is also hugely complemented by the government's new network of UK-wide Sector Skills Councils (replacing National Training Organisations NTOs). The SSCs have been created to help deliver more effectively the skills and productivity demands of both industry and business. Wide ranging measures are under way and can be explored further at **ssda.org.uk**. This includes information on the latest trailblazer SSCs that are pioneering the new service as follows:

Skillset – (broadcast, film, video and interactive media)	**skillset.org**
Lantra – (farming, agriculture, forestry and rural development)	**lantra.co.uk**
Cogent – oil, gas, chemicals manufacturing and petroleum	**cogent-ssc.com**
Skillfast – apparel, footwear and textiles	**skillfast-uk.org**
Skillsmart – retail	**brc.org.uk**

Please Note:

Until Sector Skills Councils are fully established throughout the UK, some NTO web links still feature on the following pages with many continuing to offer excellent training and careers information.

The Sites – general

Dept for Employment & Learning – Northern Ireland	**delni.gov.uk**
Future Skills Wales	**futureskillswales.com**
Investors In People	**iipuk.co.uk**
Learning & Skills Councils	**lsc.gov.uk**
Modern Apprenticeships – Scotland	**mascot.uk.com**
Modern Apprenticeships – Wales	**etod.org.uk**
Modern Apprenticeships	**realworkrealpay.info**
National Training Awards	**nationaltrainingawards.com**
Scottish Training	**sconto.org.uk**
Skillfast – Textile Footwear	**ssda.org.uk**
Skillset – Audio Visual Industry	**skillset.org**

Small Firms Training (Loans & Awards)   **lifelonglearning.co.uk/sftl**

The Sites

Education and Employment	*CLCIs AT/AV*
Community Based Learning and Development	**paulo.org.uk**
Early Years (Care)	**early-years-nto.org.uk**
Employment	**empnto.co.uk**
Further Education	**fento.org**
Higher Education	**shef.ac.uk/ucosda**

Administration, Creative, Cultural, Entertainment,

Food and Leisure	*CLCIs C/E/F/G/I*
Administration	**cfa.uk.com**
Arts and Entertainment	**metier.org.uk**
Bakery Training Council	**bakerytraining.co.uk**
Broadcast, Film, Video and Multimedia	**skillset.org**
Central Government	**central-gov-nto.org.uk**
Cleaning and Support Services	**cleaningnto.org**
Cultural Heritage	**chnto.co.uk**
Customer Service	**ics-nto.com**
E-Skills	**e-skills.com**
Food and Drink	**foodanddrinknto.org.uk**
Hairdressing and Beauty	**habia.org.uk**
Hospitality	**htf.org.uk**
Information Services	**isnto.org.uk**
Languages	**langaugesnto.org.uk**
Local Government	**lgnto.gov.uk**
Meat Training Council	**meattraining.org.uk**
Photography / Photo Imaging	**photoimagingnto.org**
Publishing	**publishingnto.co.uk**
Sports and Recreation	**sprito.org.uk**
Travel	**ttento.co.uk**

Medical, Health, Social Care, Law and Security	*CLCL's J/K/L/M*
Community Justice	**communityjusticento.co.uk**
Custodial Care	**ccnto.com**
Health	**healthwork.co.uk**
Security Industry	**sito.co.uk**
Social Services	**topss.org.uk**
Voluntary Sector	**vsnto.org.uk**

Science and Manufacturing	*CLCIs R/S/W*
Ceramic	**acdt.co.uk**
Chemical Manufacturing and Processing	**sourcerer.co.uk**
Clothing	**careers-in-clothing.co.uk**
Electricity	**eta.org.uk**
Electrotechnical Industry	**net-works.org.uk**
Engineering and Marine	**emta.org.uk/ntowsite**
Engineering Services	**esttl.org.uk**
Footwear and Leather	**flnto.com**
Furniture, Furnishings and Interiors	**ffinto.org**
Gas & Water	**ginto.co.uk**
Glass	**glass-training.co.uk**
Oil and Gas Extraction	**opito.com**
Paper	**papertrain.net**
Petroleum	**pinto.co.uk**
Pharmaceuticals	**abpi.org.uk**
Plumbing	**bpec.org.uk**
Polymers and Associated Industries	**painto.org.uk**
Print and Graphic Communication	**printnto.org**
Science, Technology and Mathematics	**stmc.org.uk**
Steel Industry	**sinto.co.uk**
Surface Coatings	**coatings.org.uk**
Telecommunications	**ntotele.com**
Textiles	**textilesnto.co.uk**

Finance, Distributions and Transport	*CLCIs N/O/Y*
Accountancy	**anto.org**
Financial Services	**fsnto.org**
British Ports	**bpit.co.uk**
Distribution	**dnto.com**
Insurance and Related Financial Services	**cii.co.uk/nto.htm**
Merchant Navy	**mntb.org.uk**
Motor Industry	**mitc.co.uk**
Passenger Transport	**transfed.org.uk**
Rail Industry Training Council	**ritc.org.uk**
Road Haulage	**rhdtc.co.uk**

Construction, Land Services, Plants and Nature	*CLCIs U/W*
Construction Industry	**citb.org.uk**
Dairy Processing and Manufacture	**dairytraining.org.uk**
Engineering Construction	**ecitb.org.uk**
Extractive and Mineral Processing	**epicnto.com**

Housing	**housingpotential.com**
Land Based Industries	**lantra.co.uk**
Property Services	**psnto.org**
Refractories and Building Products	**rbptc.co.uk**
Seafish Training	**seafish.co.uk**

Part Three

Job-Hunting

8
Job-Hunting

Getting the right job is almost an art in itself. Then the Internet comes along and increases the choice still further as just about every newspaper and recruitment agency has their vacancies on-line. Currently it is estimated that 57% of job seekers will have checked for vacancies using the Internet. Perhaps not surprising when you look at the specific careers covered in earlier chapters of this book, with many of the rated sites including specific job information and vacancy opportunities. A number of sites also offer helpful advice on CV and interview preparation. There is increasing evidence that most individuals in this new millennium will change jobs as many as eight or nine times in their working life. Increasingly, the Internet will help at such transition points, but for some it will be foolhardy to put all their trust in cyberspace for every occasion and every important decision. Personal advice and guidance is at the heart of making informed as well as appropriate choices. Careers centres, employment services and recruitment agencies, as well as family, friends and colleagues, can play a vital role in complementing and supporting the right move at the right time.

The end of this chapter (AWA–AWF) provides additional, and in many cases inspirational, sites of interest. Many are aimed at older employees, the disabled, those with learning difficulties and others who may have to adapt to working in the UK, because of changing cultural or social circumstances.

CAREER CHOICE AND CHANGE
CLCI CODES: AR–ARF

This section focuses on locating careers information, self-assessment resources and services on-line. There is increasing evidence that the process of and influences upon career decisions begins much earlier than in the past. Therefore the GCSE subject choice information at **dfes.gov.uk/whichwaynow** provides a helpful contribution to complementing early career thoughts. Then the Careers Service National Association at **careers-uk.com** helps further with excellent links to a number of key organisations and services that can help in job-seeking, careers-related information and advice. One real gem particularly worth noting for young people is **connexionscard.com** with its unique access at careers bank to the UK's largest careers directory. While it also includes late entry information for adults, more specific help is available at **worktrain. gov.uk** with more in-depth occupational information and access to vacancies held at the nation's job centres. If you're a graduate exploring postgrad courses or career opportunities, there is masses of advice and vacancy listings at **prospects.ac.uk**. It is true that few things in life are free, but senior managers may well be impressed with the support they can receive from the Career Design International at **careersnet.com**. For job-matching to specific organisations, **careersoft.co.uk** is well worth visiting. Cascaid Ltd are known for their excellent careers software products, but the word is out that careers information and accompanying photos are on their site at **cascaid.co.uk**. Careers and educational institutions may well be impressed that they can now download three different evaluation copies of psychometric programmes at **progressions.co.uk.** Further psychometric pages and tests can be located at **morrisby.co.uk**.

The Sites

Ability, Aptitude & Personality Tests	**topjobs.co.uk/ase/asetjn8.htm**
Cambridge Occupational Analysts	**coa.u-net.com**
Career Storm	**careerstorm.com**
Careers Express	**careers-express.co.uk**
Careers Service National Association	**careers-uk.com**
Careersoft	**careersoft.co.uk**
Career Tips (International)	**careertips.com**
CareerWorld UK	**careerworld.net**
Cascaid Ltd	**cascaid.co.uk**
Connexions Card	**connexionscard.com**
Enneagram Personality Dynamics (USA)	**9types.com**
InfoYouth	**infoyouth.com**
It's Your Choice – Age 16 Choices	**dfee.gov.uk/iyc**
Morrisby Organisation	**morrisby.co.uk**
On the Move – Europe	**rthj.hi.is/otm**
Progressions Ltd	**progressions.co.uk**
Self Assessment (USA)	**brain.com**
Step One – Psychometric Assessments	**step1.co.uk**
Personality: Character and Temperament (USA)	**keirsey.com**
South East Regional Information (Training and Learning)	**serif.org.uk**
Student and Graduate Advice	**prospects.ac.uk**
UK and International Guidance on the Web	**aiuto.net/ukseen.htm**
Worktrain	**worktrain.gov.uk**

CVs AND INTERVIEW PREPARATION
CLCI CODE: AVA

Personnel, as well as many business managers, are said to be delighted with the development of on-line application procedures, saving much time on already stretched administration and staffing resources. However, it may be that you are at the application end of the cycle and wanting to make your CV stand out from the pack. It is worth shopping around the Internet to see what sites are likely to complement your unique blend of experience. In fact most of the job-hunting sites listed below include help with CVs, but for starters you can always check out **cvspecial.co.uk**, **alec.co.uk** and **monster.co.uk**. Another gem is **peoplebank.co.uk** which, in addition to helping employers find the right people, acts in the interests of applicants, by hosting an easy-to-use CV-placing service. Take a look at the job seeker and create your on-line CV.

The Sites
Ask Alec	**alec.co.uk**
Bradley CVs	**bradleycvs.demon.co.uk/hotsites.htm**
CV Special	**cvspecial.co.uk**
Employment Service	**employmentservice.gov.uk**
Graduate Employment	**prospects.csu.ac.uk**
GTI Specialist Publishers (Student and Graduate)	**doctorjob.co.uk**
Jobs Times Educational Supplement	**jobs.tes.co.uk**
Royal British Legion – Ex-Servicemen and Women	**rbli.co.uk**

VACANCIES AND JOB OPPORTUNITIES
CLCI CODE: AVB

This book is not designed to include every employment and recruitment agency in the land. However, as mentioned, every effort has been made to list in the appropriate careers sections those sites that include their own jobs or vacancy pages. The selection below does include some specialist provision, but in the main focuses on general providers, specific graduate recruiters and European and international sites with opportunities for employment in the UK and overseas.

Perhaps representing the professional arm of recruitment, and a particularly useful site to employers, is the listing of member companies of the Recruitment and Employment Confederation, which can be found at **rec.uk.com**. If you are on a general job-seeking trawl, you will find most Internet providers, radio and television stations host their own vacancy listings. Some keywords to look out for may seem obvious, but you should find something within 'classifieds', 'recruitment', 'jobs', 'vacancies', 'opportunities' and 'careers' pages. **capitalfm.com** is quite a good example and like a number of other providers may draw on the same key sites such as PeopleBank, MonsterBoard and Jobsite (all listed). However, if you think you may have missed that local vacancy, then you can always try **fish4jobs.co.uk** which includes a useful location search to narrow down to specific places or distance that you are prepared to travel to for work. There is also much to entice the international job-seeker at **internationaljobs.org**. This site includes a list of organisations that have placed adverts with *International Career Employment Weekly*. Membership offers a more complete service on-line, as well as support to employers wishing to recruit from the global market-place. Alternatively, if you want to focus on Europe, why not try **eurograduate.com** or potential companies listed in the highly impressive European Business Directory at **europages.com**? This could provide your passport to opportunities on the continent, as much as securing positions with businesses in Britain who have particular market interests in the EU. Closer to home is a useful site with downloadable careers material at **insidecareers.co.uk** which represents a number of professional interests such as accountancy, logistics, management consultants, engineering, etc. A highly commendable site for undergraduate work experience is **step.org.uk**.

The Sites

Agencies, Geographical and Media

Accenture	**accenture.com**
Agency Central	**agencycentral.co.uk**
All Jobs UK Portal	**alljobsuk.com**
Brook Street	**brookstreet.co.uk**
City Jobs Worldwide	**cityjobs.com**
Daily Mail	**peoplebank.com**
Daily Telegraph	**appointments-plus.co.uk**
EmployAbility – Disabled	**nrec.org.uk/employability**
Employment Service	**employmentservice.gov.uk**
European Employment Services	**eures-jobs.com/jobs**
Financial Times	**http://ftjobs.ft.com/thejobs**
Fish 4 Jobs	**fish4jobs.co.uk**
Future Skills Wales	**futureskillswales.com**
Gis-A-Job	**gisajob.com**
Go Jobsite	**jobsite.co.uk**
Guardian	**jobsunlimited.co.uk**
International Employment Centre	**internationaljobs.org**

UK & International Jobs	**taps.co.uk**
I Don't Feel 50	**idf50.com**
I Resign	**I-resign.com**
Irish Independent Online	**independent.ie**
Irish Jobs	**exp.ie**
Irish Opportunities	**gojobsite.ie**
Irish Times	**irish-times.com**
Jobs In . . .	**jobsin.co.uk**
Jobs In Wales	**jobsinwales.com**
JobsJobsJobs	**jobsjobsjobs.co.uk**
Just People	**justpeople.com**
Job Portal to UK Sites	**jobs.co.uk**
Link to Scottish Jobs	**scotsmart.com**
Newspaper Group	**fish4jobs.co.uk**
Redundancy Help	**redundancyhelp.co.uk**
Regional, National & International Newspapers	**thepaperboy.co.uk**
Monster	**monster.co.uk**
New Deal	**newdeal.gov.uk**
Northern Ireland Jobs	**nijobs.com**
Pathfinder-One	**pathfinder-one.com**
Recruitment & Employment Confederation	**rec.uk.com**
Reed Executive	**reed.co.uk**
Retirement Matters	**retirement-matters.co.uk**
SAT UK Recruitment Portal	**recruit-online.co.uk**
Scotland Online	**recruitment.scotland.net**
Secretarial, Administrators etc.	**angelamortimer.com**
Secretarial & Office Support	**office-angels.com**
StepStone	**stepstone.com**
Times Education Supplement	**jobs.tes.co.uk**
TopJobs	**topjobs.co.uk**
Total Jobs	**totaljobs.com**
UK Learning, Training & Employment	**worktrain.gov.uk**
Workthing	**workthing.com**
World Careers Network	**wcn.co.uk**
World Service Enquiry	**wse.org.uk**

Specialist Career Portals

Accounting & Finance	**gaapweb.com**
Advertising, Broadcasting, Music & New Media	**cmoves.co.uk**
Advertising, PR Marketing & Sales	**e-job.net**
Appointments by Language	**ablrecruit.co.uk**
Appointments for Teachers	**aft.co.uk**

Architecture, Interior Design & Graphics	**networkdesign.cc**
Aupairs	**aupairs.co.uk**
Aviation, Electronics, Telecoms & Construction	**cap-recruit.co.uk**
BBC Opportunities	**bbc.co.uk/jobs**
Charity Opportunities	**charityopps.com**
Chemical Engineering	**whynotchemeng.com**
Chemistry	**chemjobs.net**
Contractor UK + IT Job Portal	**contractoruk.co.uk**
Electronic Media	**recruitmedia.co.uk**
Electronics & Software Recruitment	**e-and-s-recruitment.co.uk**
Engineers Online	**engineers-online.co.uk**
Food & Associated Industries	**foodjobs.co.uk**
Health Service Journal	**hsj.co.uk**
Hospitality, Leisure, Travel & Tourism	**careercompass.co.uk**
Hotel Staff & Professional Relief Chefs	**flourish-uk.com**
IT Jobs	**silicon.com**
IT Professionals	**4weeks.com**
Local Government Jobs	**lgcnet.com**
Nursing	**british-nursing.com**
National Health Service	**nhscareers.co.uk**
Printing & Packaging	**dotjobs.co.uk**
Public Sector Jobs	**jobsgopublic.com**
Sales & Marketing	**emrsearch.co.uk**
Science Lab Vacancies	**young-scientist.co.uk**
Security Industry	**jobsecurity.co.uk**
Shipping & Freight Industries	**topshippingjobs.co.uk**
Teaching Times	**teachingtimes.com**
UK Call Centre & Telebusiness	**telepeople.com**

Graduate Employment Opportunities

Academic & Associated Communities	**jobs.ac.uk**
Doctor Job	**doctorjob.co.uk**
EuroGraduate	**eurograduate.com**
Graduate Careers Help	**careers.lon.ac.uk**
Graduate – University of London Careers Service	**careers.lon.ac.uk**
Gradunet	**gradunet.co.uk**
Inside Careers	**insidecareers.co.uk**
MBA Jobs net	**mbajobs.net**
Milkround	**milkround.co.uk**
Prospect Web	**prospect.csu.ac.uk**
UK Graduate Careers	**get.hobsons.com**
Undergraduate Work Experience	**step.org.uk**

LABOUR MARKET INFORMATION
CLCI CODE: AVC

Labour Market Information (LMI), sometimes referred to as employment trends, is recognised by the government as an important indicator for appropriate education and employment planning and legislation. At the moment, there is great emphasis on the skills shortages as we launch into the high-tech new millennium. A more prescriptive framework, but with flexible entry to national qualifications and training, is seen as essential, if we are to compete successfully on the global stage. Lifelong learning opportunities and transferable skills are very much buzz-words. The good news is that the Internet offers us a clearer idea of work patterns and education opportunities to prepare for such change. As seen in previous chapters, we can drop in from cyberspace and explore a wealth of information sources. Many careers organisations listed in this publication have up-to-the-minute profiles on their industry: the numbers of staff, type of work and, in some cases, future employment trends. A further potentially rich source for LMI are the new Learning Skills Councils **lsc.gov.uk**, formerly known as Training and Enterprise Councils. Keep an eye on these larger regional organisations, which have the challenge of skill matching industries' needs to encouraging the provision of appropriate learning and training information. Many have, or are in the process of developing, very helpful sites. Also, don't miss checking your Careers Company (see Appendix for known web addresses), who have a history of collecting employer data, with the more innovative adding such information to their own web sites.

The Sites

CBI	**cbi.org.uk**
Centre for Labour Market Studies	**clms.le.ac.uk**
European Information (Education / Professional / LMI)	**estia.educ.goteborg.se**
Future Skills Wales	**futureskillswales.com**
Government Portal LMI	**dfee.gov.uk / datasphere**
Graduate Labour Market	**prospects.csu.ac.uk / student / cidd / lmi**
Henley Centre	**henleycentre.co.uk**
Higher Education Statistics Agency	**hesa.ac.uk**
The Institute for Employment Studies	**employment-studies.co.uk**
Institute of Employment Research	**warwick.ac.uk / IER**
Joseph Rowntree Foundation	**jrf.org.uk / knowledge / findings**
Learning and Skills Councils	**lsc.gov.uk**
LMI Research	**lmi-research.co.uk**

National Foundation for Educational Research	**nfer.ac.uk**
National Statistics – Offical UK Sites	**statistics.gov.uk**
Northern Ireland Statistics & Research Agency	**nisra.gov.uk**
Policy Studies Institute	**psi.org.uk**
The Scottish Council for Research in Education	**scre.ac.uk**
Scottish Enterprise Network	**scottish-enterprise.com**
Sector Skills Councils	**ssda.org.uk**
Social Science Gateway – LMI	**sosig.ac.uk**

SELF-EMPLOYMENT AND VOLUNTARY WORK
CLCI CODE: AVD

Research from the independent Policy Studies Institute reports that there are an increasing number of unemployed people venturing into self-employment, from 17% in the 1980s to 40% in 1993. Careers companies can offer advice and information, while Local Agencies and Learning and Skills Councils (see above) at **lsc.gov.uk** are certainly worth exploring. Like so many services the quality of help and advice can vary, but speaking from personal experience, I have benefited from exceptional professional help from my local borough Business Link Advice Centre. Free, in confidence consultation, and introductory self-employment courses will help you decide whether your ideas are worth the risk. There is also tremendous help on-line with some new, as well as established sites such as **businesslink.org** and **smallbusinessadvice.org.uk**

In contrast, voluntary organisations are plentiful on the web, with opportunities to volunteer for just about any activity in almost any part of the world. To get a feel for some of the organisations involved in voluntary work, check out the superb Gateway Links pages at **ncvo-vol.org.uk** and the A–Z listing, which will take you directly to the home pages of over 600 voluntary organisations.

The Sites

Barnardo's	**barnardos.org.uk**
Business Link	**businesslink.org**
Charity Choice	**charitychoice.co.uk**
Charity Commission	**charity-commission.gov.uk**
Childline UK	**childline.org.uk**
International Voluntary Service	**ivsgbn.demon.co.uk**
National Centre for Volunteering	**volunteering.org.uk**
National Council of Voluntary Organisations	**ncvo-vol.org.uk**
The Prince's Trust	**princes-trust.org.uk**
The Samaritans	**samaritans.org.uk**

The Scout Association	**scoutbase.org.uk**
Small Business Advice	**smallbusinessadvice.org.uk**
Voluntary Organisations Internet Server	**vois.org.uk**
Voluntary Service Overseas	**vso.org.uk**
Voluntary Work	**csv.org.uk**
Work Experience USA	**workexperienceusa.com**
Worldwide Volunteering	**worldwidevolunteering.org.uk**
World Service Enquiry	**wse.org.uk**
Young Enterprise	**young-enterprise.org.uk**

EMPLOYMENT RIGHTS AND UNEMPLOYMENT
CLCI CODES: AVF–AVH

If you have ever wondered what exactly your employment rights are, then a good place to explore is the Department of Trade and Industry at **dti.gov.uk** where you can search for information on employment legislation. You can also check out the employment pages at the Citizens' Advice Bureau site at **adviceguide.org.uk**. The Low Pay Commission at **lowpay.gov.uk** provides helpful details on the recommendations made to government on the National Minimum Wage. For a wider appreciation of all the issues related to low pay and bad employment practice, visit the West Midlands Low Pay Unit's very informative pages at **wmlowpay.org.uk**. The Department of Work and Pensions at **dwp.gov.uk** has everything you need to know about entitlements to money, child support, war pensions and even helpful information if you are planning to live abroad. There is little doubt that the combined forces of technology and the ever competing global market-place make for a very uncertain employment future. Many of us are no longer so secure in our personal and professional skills. And yet the opportunities for lifelong learning as well as developing new and more transferable skills have never been better. Leaf back through the pages to the education, training and self-employment topics, but also be hugely encouraged by checking out some real site gems at I Don't Feel 50! **idf50.co.uk**, **redundancyhelp.co.uk** and **i-resign.com**

The Sites

British Employment Law	**emplaw.co.uk**
Croner (publications on employment law etc.)	**croner.co.uk**
Department of Work and Pensions	**dwp.gov.uk**
Department for Employment & Learning – Northern Ireland	**delni.gov.uk**
Employment Relations	**dti.gov.uk**
Employment Service	**employmentservice.gov.uk**

I Don't Feel 50	**idf50.co.uk**
I Resign	**i-resign.com**
Low Pay Commission	**lowpay.gov.uk**
New Deal	**newdeal.gov.uk**
Redundancy Help	**redundancyhelp.co.uk**
Retirement Matters – 50+	**retirement-matters.co.uk**
West Midlands Low Pay Unit	**wmlowpay.org.uk**
Workplace Bullying	**successunlimited.co.uk/bully**

ADDITIONAL INFORMATION FOR SPECIFIC GROUPS
CLCI CODE: AWA

SAGA Magazine is mainly written for those over 50 and is the second largest subscription magazine in the UK. Previous archive material can be viewed at **saga.co.uk**. Also recommended is Paul Lewis's site, with articles written for SAGA on financial and consumer rights for older people. He has numerous informative pages, but you will need to search 'latest writing' at **paullewis.co.uk**. If it's equality you are looking for, then check out the Equal Opportunities Commission pages at **eoc.org.uk**. There is plenty of helpful advice on anything from press releases to sexual discrimination and employment law. The link pages also have a great European and international feel, which may well be useful for students researching similar organisations overseas. You may have already discovered the joys of lifelong learning, but there are contacts out there which are particularly suited to older learners, such as those involved with the University of the Third Age and found at **u3a.org.uk**.

The Sites

Age Concern	**ace.org.uk**
Ageism	**agepositive.gov.uk**
Age Net	**agenet.ac.uk**
BBC Education Learning Zone	**bbc.co.uk/education/lzone**
Equal Opportunities Commission	**eoc.org.uk**
National Grid for Learning	**ngfl.gov.uk**
SAGA Editorial	**paullewis.co.uk**
SAGA Magazine	**saga.co.uk**
Silver Surfers	**silversurfers.co.uk**
Silver Surfers Net	**silversurfers.net**
Training Access Points (NW England)	**tap.co.uk**
Training Standards Council	**tsc.gov.uk**
University of the Third Age (every public library has access)	**u3a.org.uk**
Women's International Centre	**wic.org**

HEALTH PROBLEMS AND DISABILITIES
CLCI CODE: AWB

It is encouraging to see just how much the Internet can help on almost any health-related issue. Radar is the Royal Association for Disability and Rehabilitation, an organisation that represents the needs, views and wishes of over 8.3 million people. Their web site at **radar.org.uk** is packed with helpful advice and information. However, if you are more concerned with how the IT revolution may assist in your particular circumstances, but have no idea where to start, check out the home page of **disability.gov.uk** and the link to the government's Web Accessibility Initiative. The contents could be more user-friendly, but are still informative and complemented nicely by **ability.org.uk**. If you want to keep up with all the disability issues, excellent information can be found at **disabilitynow.org.uk** which has a superb links page accessing a wealth of amazing sites on anything from sport and the arts to education and transport. A site which can be highly recommended for disabled students is **skill.org.uk** which includes excellent information on applying to further and higher education, finance, and getting into full employment.

Have you ever wondered whether sign language is universal? Discover this and much more by visiting the British Deaf Association at **bda.org.uk**. There is also an amazing US site for the deaf (which is thought to be the largest deaf web site in the world) at **handspeak.com** with a host of topical and informative detail on deafness-related issues. Another first-rate site, this time for the visually impaired, is run by the Royal National Institute for the Blind at **rnib.org.uk**. There is much to commend, but their Age 11–16 pages are packed with excellent material, and the *Spotlight Magazine* is particularly useful for identifying tapes, large print and Braille resources. The Internet has also opened up new opportunities for open and distance learning so do check Dorton College's offerings at **dorton-coll.ac.uk**. There is little doubt that today's drug culture, with its impact on the young and vulnerable, as well as increasing drug dependency, is a major concern. For objective, accurate and current information on all aspects of drug misuse, visit the Druscrope at **drugscope.org.uk**. If you are looking for work, there is some very helpful advice at **opportunities.org.uk**, but do not neglect any of the careers sites listed throughout this book. It is true that specific disabilities, which we all have to some extent, will limit certain career aspirations, but the more astute companies and organisations recognise the exceptional loyalty and valuable contribution the disabled can and do make to their success.

The Sites

The Ability Project	**ability.org.uk**
Alcohol Concern	**alcoholconcern.org.uk**
British Deaf Association	**britishdeafassociation.org.uk**
British Epilepsy Association	**epilepsy.org.uk**
Cerebral Palsy	**scope.org.uk**
Charity Choice	**charitychoice.co.uk**
Connections Disability Scotland	**connections.gcal.ac.uk**
Contact a Family	**cafamily.org.uk**
Cystic Fibrosis Trust	**cftrust.org.uk**
Deafblindness	**sense.org.uk**
Depression Alliance	**depressionalliance.org.uk**
Disabled Access – London	**accesslondon.co.uk**
Disability	**disability.gov.uk**
Disability Net	**disabilitynet.co.uk**
Disability Now Newspaper	**disabilitynow.org.uk**
Disability Zone	**bbc.co.uk/radio4/progs/genre/genre_disability.shtml**
Drugscope	**drugscope.org.uk**
Employability	**nrec.org.uk/employability**
Employment Opportunities	**opportunities.org.uk**
Epilepsy and Employment	**epilepsy.org.uk**
Guide Dogs for the Blind Association	**gdba.org.uk**
Handspeak (US)	**handspeak.com**
National Autistic Society	**oneworld/org/autism_uk**
National Bureau for Students with Disabilities	**skill.org.uk**
National Centre for Children and Young People with Epilepsy	**stpiers.org.uk**
Royal Association for Disability and Rehabilitation	**radar.org.uk**
Royal London Society for the Blind	**dorton-coll.ac.uk**
Royal National Institute for the Blind	**rnib.org.uk**
Soundsense Community Music	**soundsense.org**
Trashed – Drugs Information	**trashed.co.uk**

LEARNING DIFFICULTIES
CLCI CODE: AWC

In the past, for many individuals now known to have had dyslexia, school life was just a humiliation, but now all children going through primary education are diagnosed and helped with what is recognised as a very common ailment. Visit any one of the sites listed below, especially the British Dyslexia Association at **bda-dyslexia.org.uk** where excellent information can be found. When it comes to information on topics relating to special educational needs, one of the best is to be found in the USA at **seriweb.com**. This is an excellent resource, covering a range of topics from behaviour disorders and autism to teaching the gifted and talented. Research students investigating deep-rooted social issues on matters such as poor housing, low pay, unemployment and high crime rates will benefit from checking out the government's own Social Exclusion Unit pages at **cabinet-office.gov.uk/seu**.

The Sites

British Dyslexia Association	**bda-dyslexia.org.uk**
Central Suffolk District Dyslexia Association	**dyslexia.org.uk**
Davis Dyslexia Association International	**dyslexia.com**
National Association for Special Education Needs	**nasen.org.uk**
Resources for Special Needs	**dfes.gov.uk/specialneeds**
Severe Learning Difficulties	**equals.co.uk**
Social Exclusion Unit	**cabinet-office.gov.uk/seu**
Special Education Resources on the Internet (US)	**web.com**
Workforce – Special Needs	**workforce.org.uk**

ETHNIC MINORITIES AND REFUGEES
CLCI CODES: AWD–AWE

There are particular sites worthy of recommendation on matters relating to ethnic minority or racial issues. The Commission for Racial Equality at **cre.gov.uk** can advise on racial discrimination, harassment or abuse. Their news release service is also a good way of keeping in touch. The site map of the Equal Opportunities Commission at **eoc.org.uk** is helpful, as you can then link to particular concerns such as employment law, or European and international human rights issues. If you have queries about immigration or foreign affairs, check out the new Immigration Advisory Service web site at **iasuk.org**.

The Sites

Asylum Support	**asylumsupport.info**
Black Britain	**blackbritain.co.uk**
Commission for Racial Equality	**cre.gov.uk**
Equal Opportunities Commission	**eoc.org.uk**
Ethnic Pages	**ethnic-pages.co.uk**
Immigration Advisory Service	**iasuk.org**
Joint Council for the Welfare of Immigrants	**jewi.org.uk**
Refugee Council	**refugeecouncil.org.uk**
Scottish Refugee Council	**scottishrefugeecouncil.org.uk**

Worldwide Refugee Information (USA)   **refugees.org**

OFFENDERS AND EX-OFFENDERS
CLCI CODE: AWF

Most of the sites listed below and others can be traced to the link pages of HM Prison Service at **hmprisonservice.gov.uk**. To get an understanding of how release decisions are directed by the Home Secretary, go to **paroleboard.gov.uk**. There is also the Criminal Cases Review Commission site at **ccrc.gov.uk** who are the independent body responsible for investigating suspected miscarriages of criminal justice. A list of organisations and charities that help the ex-offender to integrate back into society can be found at **hmprisonservice.gov.uk/assistance**. However, it is NACRO, the National Association for the Care and Resettlement of Offenders at **nacro.org**, which is well known for its housing and training workshops.

The Sites

Crime Concern	**crimeconcern.org.uk**
Crime Reduction Toolkit	**crimeeducation.gov.uk**
Criminal Cases Review Commission	**ccrc.gov.uk**
Disclosure – England & Wales	**disclosure.gov.uk**
Disclosure – Scotland	**scro.police.uk/discscot.htm**
Divert	**divert.org**
Ex-Offenders	**apextrust.com**
Help for Prisoners, Ex-Offenders and Families	**hmprisonservice.gov.uk/assistance**
National Association for the Care and Resettlement of Offenders	**nacro.org**
The Parole Board for England and Wales	**paroleboard.gov.uk**
Prisoner's Education	**prisonerseducation.org**
Safeguarding Communities – Scotland	**sacro.org.uk**
Victim Support	**victimsupport.com**
Youth Justice Board	**youth-justice-board.gov.uk**

Appendix:
Further Useful Web Sites

CAREERS SERVICES, TRAINING AND EDUCATION AGENCIES AND SERVICES
CLCI CODES: AXA–AXC

The Sites

Careers Journal International	**careers-journal.com**
Careers Scotland	**careers-scotland.org.uk**
Careers Wales	**careerswales.com**
Careers Service National Association	**careers-uk.com**
Connexions Service	**connexions.gov.uk**
Dept for Employment & Learning – Northern Ireland	**delni.gov.uk**
Institute of Career Guidance	**icg-uk.org**
International Careers Journal	**careers-cafe.com**
Learning and Skills Councils	**lcs.gov.uk**
Scottish Enterprise Network	**scottishenterprise.com**
Sector Skills Development Agency	**ssda.org.uk**

CAREER COMPANIES

Channel Islands

Guernsey Careers Service	**gcs.gov.gg**
Jersey Careers Service	**jcs.co.je**

England

Calderdale & Kirklees Careers Service Partnership Ltd	**workabout.org**
Capital Careers	**capitalcareers.ltd.uk**
Careers and Education Business Partnership	**cebp.co.uk**
Careers Bradford Ltd	**careersb.co.uk**
Careers Essex	**careersessex.co.uk**
Careers Management (Buckingham, The City, Islington, Hackney, Kent, Hampshire, Isle of Wight, Surrey, West Sussex	**careers.co.uk**

Careers Management Futures	**futures-careers.co.uk**
Careers Partnership	**careerspartnership.co.uk**
CfBT Advice & Guidance	**wayahead-careers.co.uk**
Connexions Birmingham and Solihull	**connexions-bs.co.uk**
Connexions Bournemouth Dorset and Poole	**connexions-bdp.co.uk**
Connexions Cambridgeshire and Peterborough Ltd	**connexionscp.co.uk**
Connexions Cheshire and Warrington	**connexions-cw.co.uk**
Connexions Cornwall and Devon	**careers-cd.org.uk**
Connexions County Durham	**connexions-durham.org**
Connexions Coventry & Warwickshire	**connexions-covandwarks.org.uk**
Connexions Cumbria	**connexionscumbria.co.uk**
Connexions Derbyshire	**connexions-derbyshire.org**
Connexions Greater Merseyside	**connexions-gmerseyside.co.uk**
Connexions Herefordshire & Worcestershire	**connexions-hw.org.uk**
Connexions Lancashire Ltd	**lancashire-connexions.org.uk**
Connexions Lincolnshire and Rutland	**connexions-lincsandrutland.co.uk**
Connexions Nottingham	**cnxnotts.co.uk**
Connexions Shropshire Telford & Wrekin	**connexionsstw.org.uk**
Connexions Somerset	**connexions-somerset.org.uk**
Connexions Staffordshire	**cxstaffs.co.uk**
Connexions Suffolk	**thesource.me.uk**
Connexions Tees Valley	**connexionsteesvalley.co.uk**
Connexions Tyne and Wear	**connexions-tw.co.uk**
Connexions West of England	**connexionswest.org.uk**
Connexions West Yorkshire	**wyzup.net**
Guidance Enterprises Group	**guidance-enterprises.co.uk**
Hertfordshire Careers Services Ltd	**herts-careers.co.uk**
Humberside Partnership	**getting-on.co.uk**
Leicestershire Careers and Guidance Services	**leicester-careers.co.uk**
Lifetime Careers, Bolton, Bury & Rochdale	**lifetime-careers.co.uk/bbr**
Lifetime Careers (Brent and Harrow)	**careers-london.com**
Lifetime Careers, Wiltshire Ltd	**lifetime-careers.co.uk/lcw**
Lifetime Careers Ltd (Barnsley, Doncaster, and Rotherham)	**lifetime-careers.co.uk/bdr**
Lifetime Careers Ltd (Stockport and High Peak)	**lifetime-careers.co.uk**
London South Bank Careers	**lsbcareers.co.uk**
Norfolk Careers Services Ltd	**norfolk-careers.co.uk**
Prospects Careers Services (East London & Central London, South London, North London and Black Country)	**prospects.co.uk**
Sheffield Futures	**connexionsinsheffield.org.uk**

Sussex Careers Services	**sussexcareers.co.uk**
Wakefield District Guidance Services	**guidance-enterprises.co.uk**
Wigan Careers Service Ltd	**wigan-careers.org.uk**

Northern Ireland

Careers and Occupational Information Unit	**teaonline.gov.uk**
Department for Employment and Learning	**delni.gov.uk**

Scotland

Careers Scotland	**careers-scotland.org.uk**
Career Development, Edinburgh and Lothians	**cdel.co.uk**
Career Development, Edinburgh and Lothians adults	**adultguidance.co.uk**
Careers Central Ltd	**careers-central.com**
Dumfries and Galloway Careers Service	**careers-scotland.org.uk**
Dunbartonshire and Lomond Careers Service Ltd	**dlcsp.org.uk**
Fife Careers	**fifedirect.org.uk**
Glasgow	**glasgow-careers.org.uk**
Glasgow Adult Guidance Network	**glasgow-agn.org.uk**
Grampian Education Business Partnership	**sstn.co.uk**
Highland Careers Services Ltd	**highlandcareers.co.uk**
Lanarkshire Careers	**o2b.org.uk**
The Network for Adult Guidance Tayside	**nagt.co.uk**
Renfrewshire Careers Partnership Ltd	**renfrewshire-careers.co.uk**
Shetland Careers Service Ltd	**shetland-careers.org.uk**

Wales

Careers Wales	**careerswales.com**
Careers Wales Cardiff & Vale	**cardiffandvale.org.uk**
Careers Wales Gwent	**careerswalesgwent.org.uk**
Careers Wales North East	**careersplus.co.uk**
Careers Wales North West	**gyrfa.org.uk**
Careers Wales Powys	**careerswales.powys.org.uk**
Careers Wales West	**careerswaleswest.co.uk**

LOCAL, NATIONAL, INTERNATIONAL DIRECTORIES AND AGENCIES, PERSONAL SUPPORT SERVICES
CLCI CODES: AXD–AXG

The Sites

British Association for Counselling	**bac.co.uk**
British Quality Foundation	**quality-foundation.co.uk**

Career Tips – International	**careertips.com**
Central Office of Information	**coi.gov.uk**
Department for Education and Skills	**dfes.gov.uk**
Department of Education for Northern Ireland	**deni.gov.uk**
Department of Trade and Industry	**dti.gov.uk**
EU Institutions	**europa.eu.int**
European Information	
(Education/Professional/LMI)	**estia.educ.goteborg.se**
General Teaching Council for Scotland	**gtcs.org.uk**
Government Departments	**ukonline.gov.uk**
Housing Corporation	**housingcorp.gov.uk**
International Training and Education Conference	**itec.gov.uk**
Investors in People	**iipuk.co.uk**
London Office of European Commission	**cec.org.uk**
National Association of Citizens Advice Bureaux	**nacab.org.uk**
National Grid For Learning	**ngfl.gov.uk**
Northern Ireland Information	**globalgateway.com**
Northern Ireland Public Service Web	**nics.gov.uk**
Office of Fair Trading	**oft.gov.uk**
OFSTED	**ofsted.gov.uk**
Public Broadcasting Service Online	**pbs.org**
Scottish Council for Educational Technology	**itscotland.com**
Tradepartners UK	**tradepartners.gov.uk**
Welsh Development Agency	**wda.co.uk**
Workers' Educational Association	**wea.org.uk**
UK & International Guidance on the Web	**aiuto.met/ukseen.htm**
United Nations Information Centre	**un.org**

CAREERS EDUCATION AND GUIDANCE
CLCI CODE: AQA

The Sites

BECTA	**becta.org.uk.careersict**
Careers and Education in Scotland	**ceg.org.uk**
Careers Education & Guidance Net	**cegnet.co.uk**
Careers Wales	**careerswales.com**
Council on International Educational Exchange	**ciee.org**
National Association of Careers and Guidance Teachers	**nacgt.org.uk**
NGFL Career Development	**http://careers.ngfl.gov.uk**
University of Northumbria	
– link to over 300 CEG sites	**unn.ac.uk/academic/hswe/careers**

CAREERS LIBRARY RESOURCES
CLCI CODE: AQD

The Sites
Cambridge Occupational Analysts – software	**coa.co.uk**
Careers Europe – software	**careerseurope.co.uk**
Careersoft – software	**careersoft.co.uk**
Careers Research and Advisory Centre / NICEC	**crac.org.uk**
Cascaid – software	**cascaid.co.uk**
Connexions Card	**connexionscard.gov.uk**
Copyright Website	**benedict.com**
Europe in the Round – software	**gesvt.com**
Hobsons CRAC	**hobsons.co.uk**
How To Books Ltd	**howtobooks.co.uk**
HighFlyers Publishing Ltd	**highflyerspublishing.co.uk**
Independent Schools Careers Organisation	**isco.org.uk**
JIIG-CAL Progressions – software	**progressions.co.uk**
Kogan Page	**kogan-page.co.uk**
Lifetime Careers Wiltshire	**lifetime-publishing.co.uk**
McGraw-Hill Publishing Company (UK / USA)	**mcgraw-hill.co.uk**
Network Educational Press	**networkpress.co.uk**
Pearson Publishing	**pearson.co.uk**
Peterson's (USA)	**petersons.com**
School Government Publishing Company Ltd	**schoolgovernment.co.uk**
Surf In2 Careers	**surfin2careers.com**
Trotman Group	**careers-portal.com**
Worldwide Volunteering – software	**worldwidevolunteering.org.uk**

EDUCATION, EMPLOYMENT RESEARCH
CLCI CODES: AQF-AQG

The Sites
Centre for Labour Market Studies	**clms.le.ac.uk**
Graduate Labour Market	**prospects.csu.ac.uk / student / cidd / lmi**
Henley Centre	**henleycentre.co.uk**
High Education Statistics Agency	**hesa.ac.uk**
The Institute for Employment Studies	**employment-studies.co.uk**
Institute of Employment Research	**warwick.ac.uk / IER**
Joseph Rowntree Foundation	**jrf.org.uk / knowledge / findings**
National Foundation for Educational Research	**nfer.ac.uk**
Policy Studies Institute	**psi.org.uk**
School and College Performance Tables	**dfee.gov.uk / perform.htm**

The Scottish Council for Research in Education   scre.ac.uk

SOCIAL ISSUES
CLCI CODE: AQH

The Sites

Age Concern	**ace.org.uk**
Bullying in the Workplace	**successunlimited.co.uk**
Bullying Online	**bullying.co.uk**
Care for the Family	**cff.org.uk**
Centrepoint	**centrepoint.org.uk**
Contact a Family	**cafamily.org.uk**
Couple Counselling – Scotland	**couplecounselling.org**
Drugscope	**drugscope.org.uk**
Drug Misuse Scotland	**drugmisuse.isdscotland.org**
Homelessness	**housingcorp.gov.uk**
Homelessness Pages	**homelessnesspages.org.uk**
Housing – Northern Ireland	**nihe.gov.uk**
I Don't Feel 50!	**idf50.co.uk**
Low Pay Unit	**lowpay.gov.uk**
Mental Health	**mind.org.uk**
National Centre for Social Research	**natcen.ac.uk**
National Family Mediation	**nfm.u-net.com**
NCH Action for Children	**nchafc.org.uk**
Redundancy Help	**redundancyhelp.co.uk**
Retirement Matters	**retirement-matters.co.uk**
Shelter	**shelter.org**
Student Debt	**studentdebt.org.uk**
Turning Point	**turning-point.co.uk**
UK Foyer Federation Network	**foyer.net**
UK Parents Online	**ukparents.co.uk**
Wrecked	**wrecked.co.uk**

Citizenship, Inclusion & Social Action

Caring Matters	**caringmatters.dial.pipex.com**
Centre for Economic & Social Inclusion	**uuy.org.uk**
Centre for Studies on Inclusion education	**http://inclusion.uwe.ac.uk**
Citizens Connect	**citizensconnection.net**
Citizenship – Education	**dfes.gov.uk/citizenship**
Common Purpose	**commonpurpose.org.uk**
Community Action Network	**can-online.org.uk**

Demos – Think Tank	**demos.co.uk**
Include	**include.org.uk**
National Curriculum – Citizenship	**nc.uk.net**
Social Exclusion Unit	**cabinet-office.gov.uk/seu**

Job Index

The first page numbers direct you to the appropriate introductory section of the book. Wherever possible page numbers then lead you to specific job titles. However, with much overlap in sites as well as information sometimes listed within 'other sites of interest', it may be necessary to broaden your area of search. See also pages 143–156 when looking for appropriate job hunting sites.